Maths
made easy

Key Stage 1
ages 5-6
Beginner

Author
Sue Phillips

Consultant
Sean McArdle

LONDON • NEW YORK • MUNICH • MELBOURNE • DELHI

Numbers

Trace the numbers.

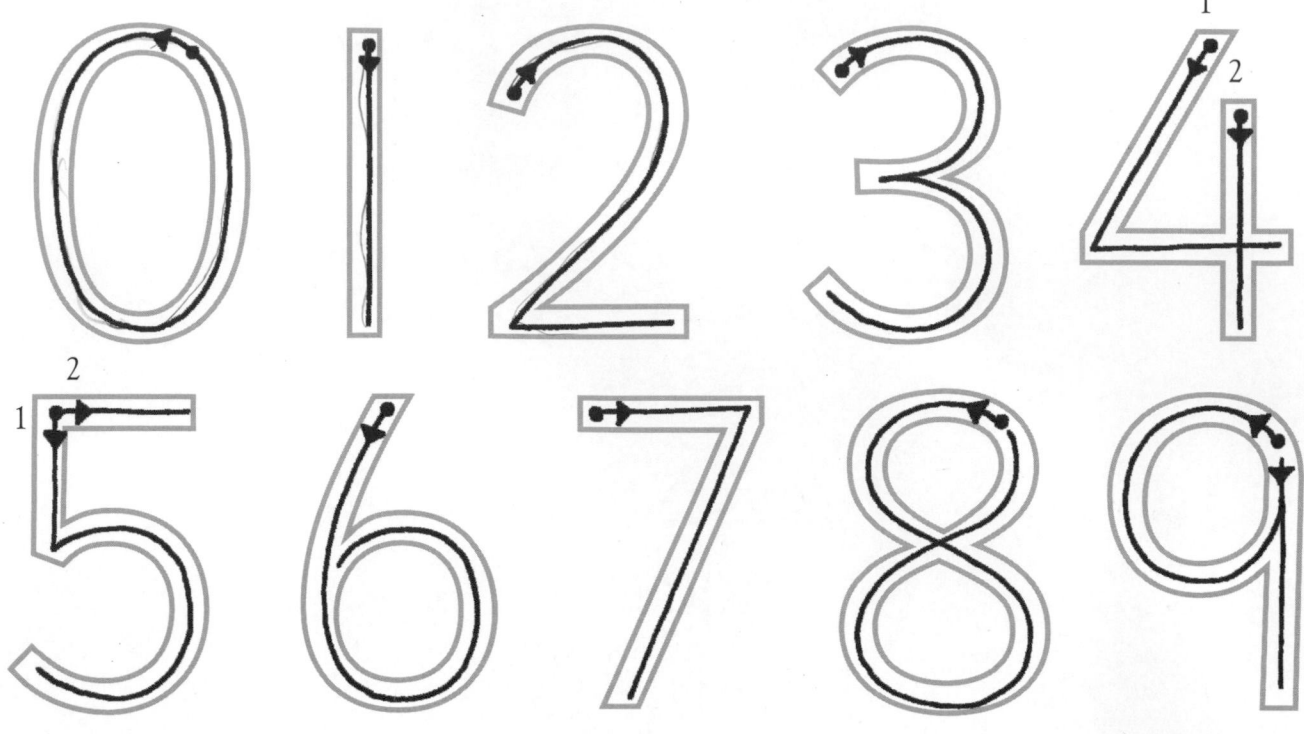

Write the numbers.

0 0 0 0 0 0 0

1 1 1 1 1 1 1

2 2 2 2 2 2 2

3 3 3 3 3 3 3

4 4 4 4 4 4 4

5 5 5 5 5 5 5

6 6 6 6 6 6 6

7 7 7 7 7 7 7

8 8 8 8 8 8 8

9 9 9 9 9 9 9

Numbers and pictures

Count the animals, draw the dots, and write the number.

🐌🐌	2	[domino]	.... two
🪲🪲🪲	3	3 0	✓ three
🐜🐜🐜🐜🐜	5	5 0	✓ five
🐜🐜🐜🐜🐜🐜	6	6 0	✓ six

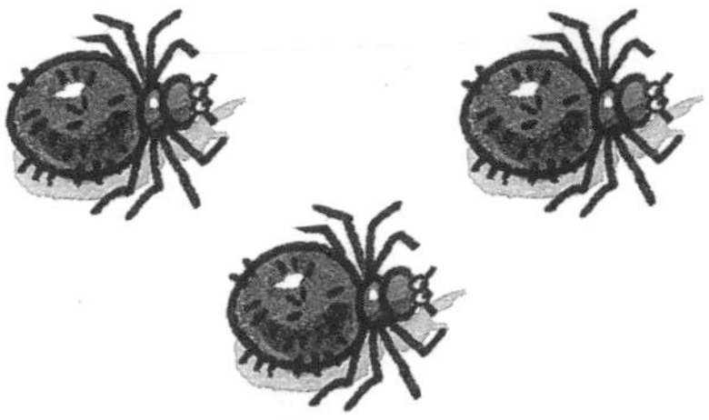

Draw your own examples.

houses	7	0 7	✓ seven
scribble	1	1 0	one

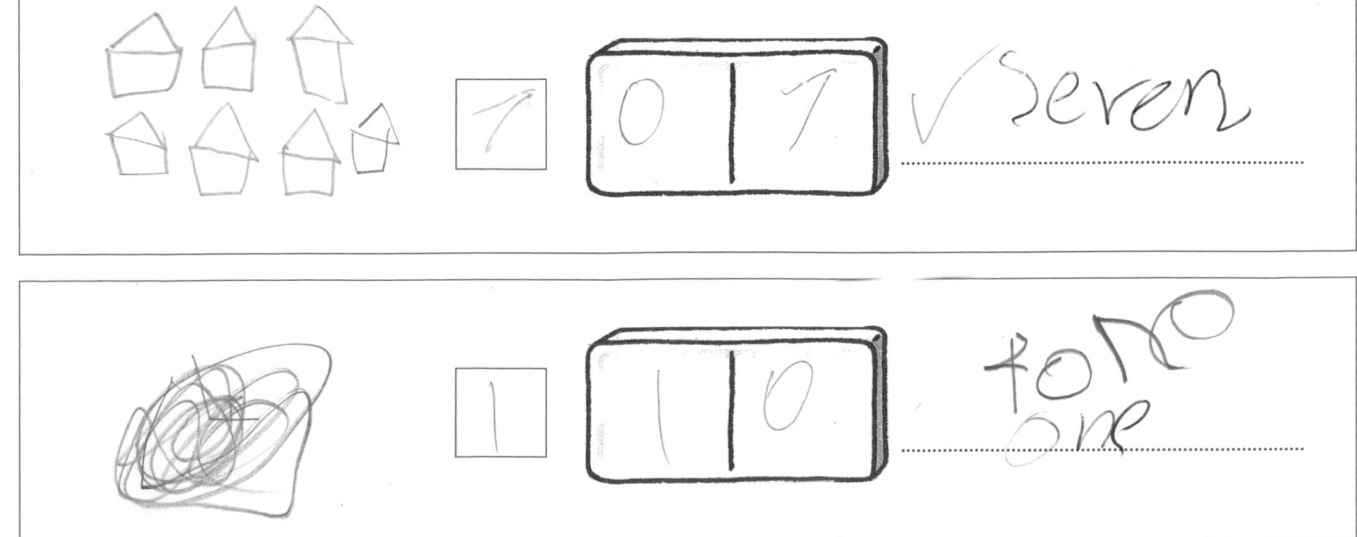

Counting

Join the set to the number.

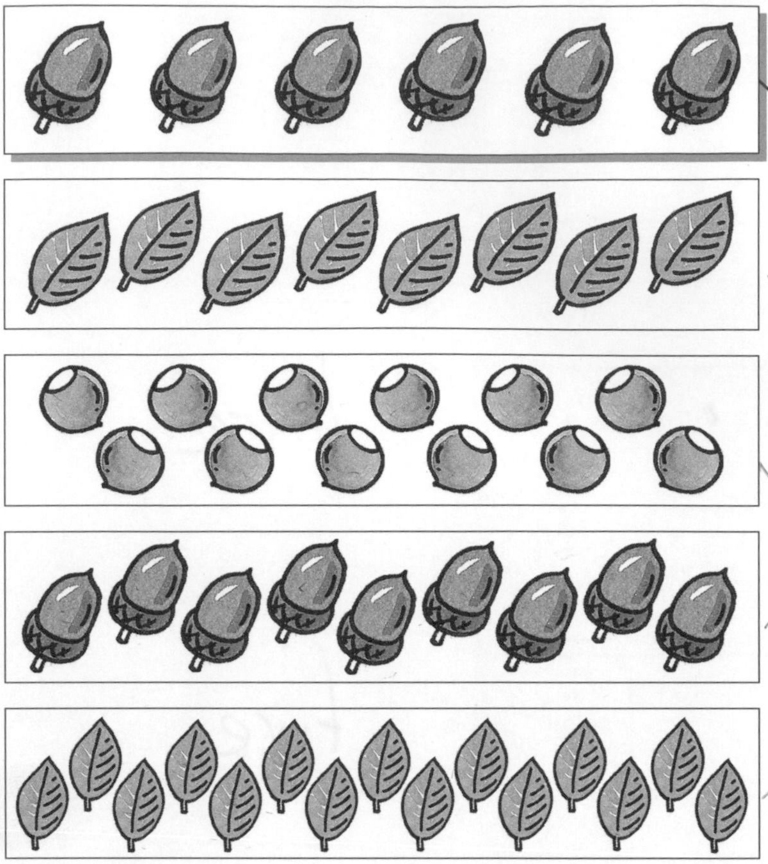

8

9

6

15

10

12

Draw your own example.

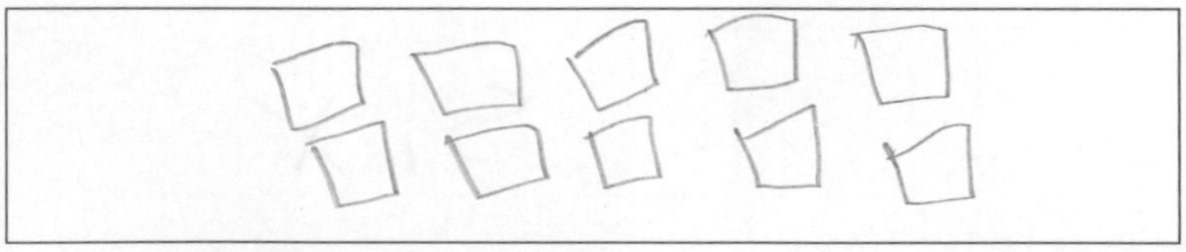

Count the beads.

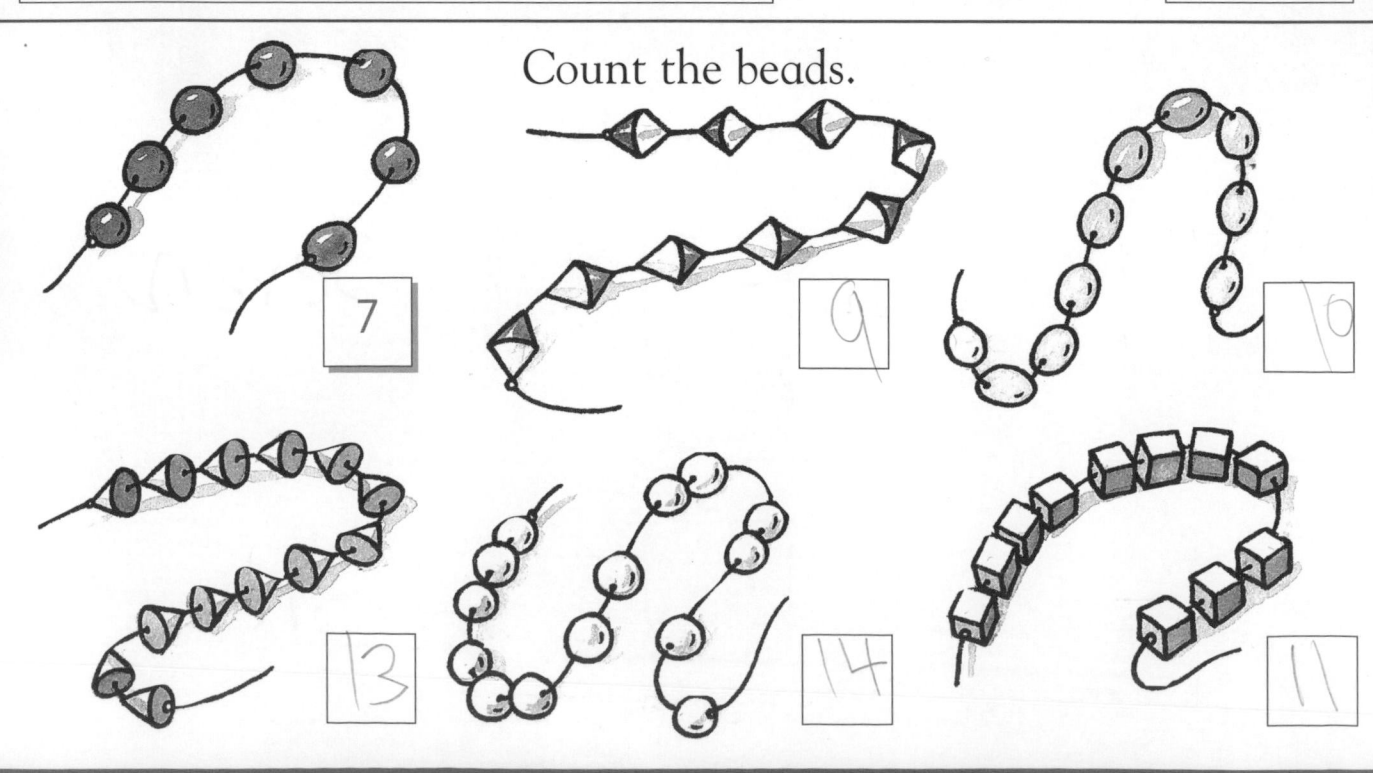

7

9

10

13

14

11

Counting out loud

Say and write the missing numbers.

Missing numbers

Write in the missing numbers.

Number bonds

Colour some of the fish red, and write the numbers in the boxes.

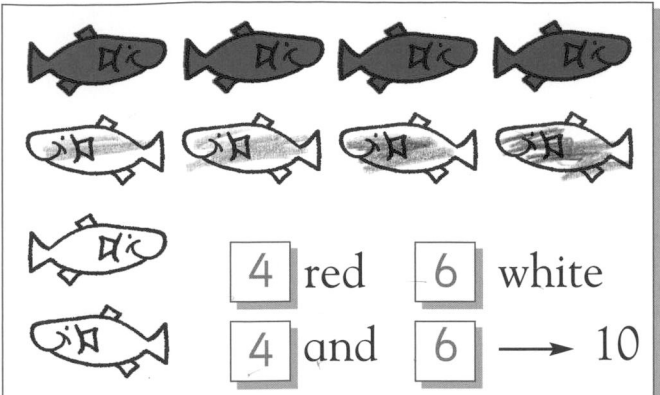

4 red   6 white
4 and   6 ⟶ 10

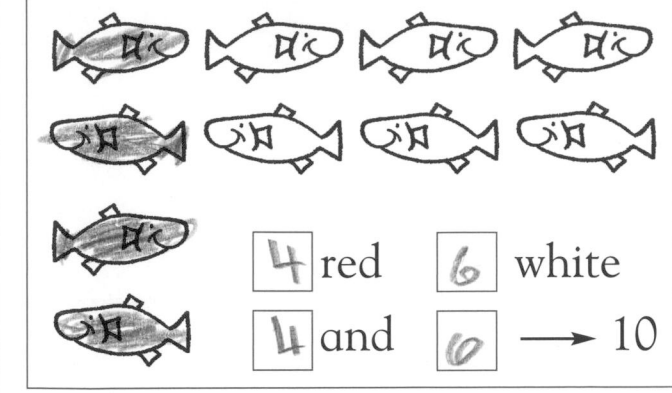

4 red   6 white
4 and   6 ⟶ 10

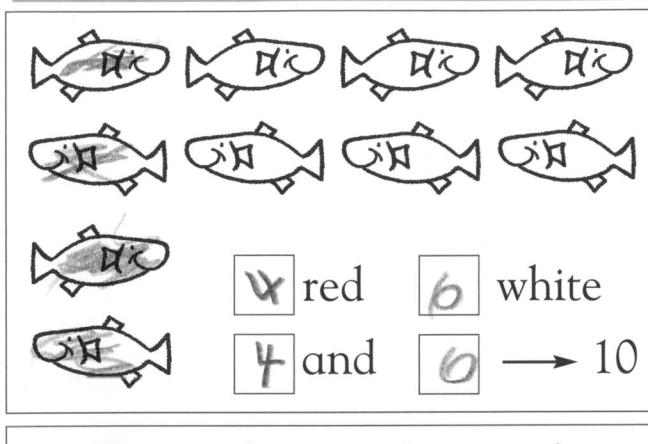

4 red   6 white
4 and   6 ⟶ 10

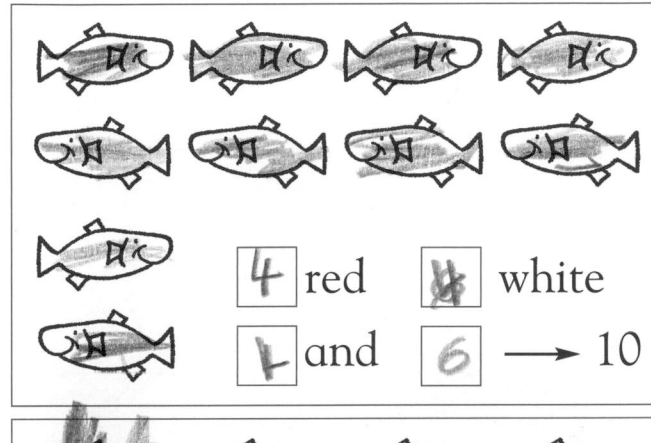

4 red   4 white
4 and   6 ⟶ 10

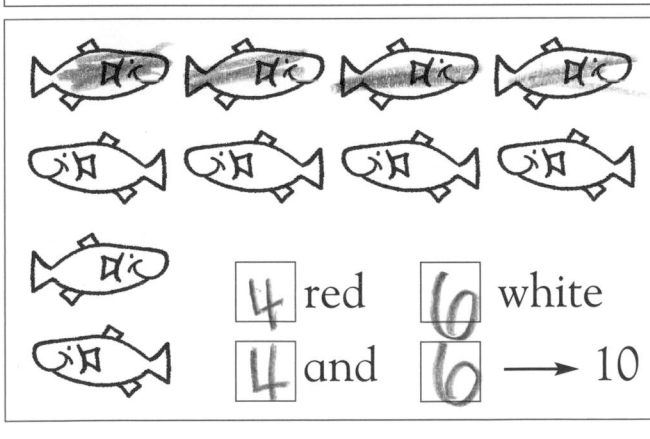

4 red   6 white
4 and   6 ⟶ 10

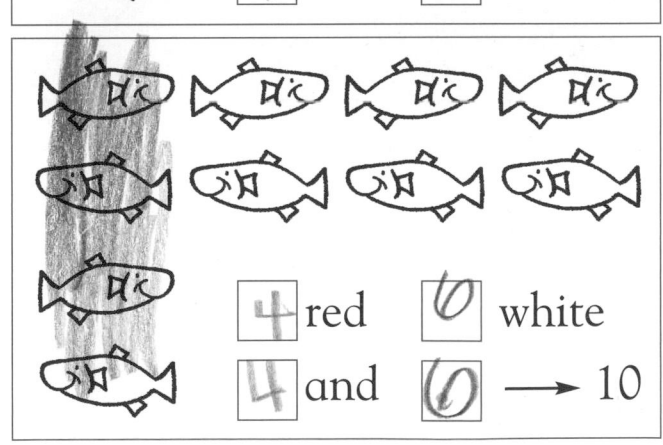

4 red   0 white
4 and   0 ⟶ 10

Write the missing numbers in the boxes to make 10.

10 and   0 ⟶ 10   6 and   4 ⟶ 10   2 and   8 ⟶ 10

9 and   1 ⟶ 10   5 and   5 ⟶ 10   1 and   9 ⟶ 10

8 and   2 ⟶ 10   4 and   6 ⟶ 10   0 and   10 ⟶ 10

7 and   3 ⟶ 10   3 and   7 ⟶ 10

Count in 10s

Match the numbers to the words.

| fifty | ten | thirty | twenty | forty |

| 10 | 20 | 30 | 40 | 50 | 60 | 70 | 80 | 90 | 100 |

| seventy | ninety | sixty | eighty | one hundred |

Which numbers has the snail hidden?

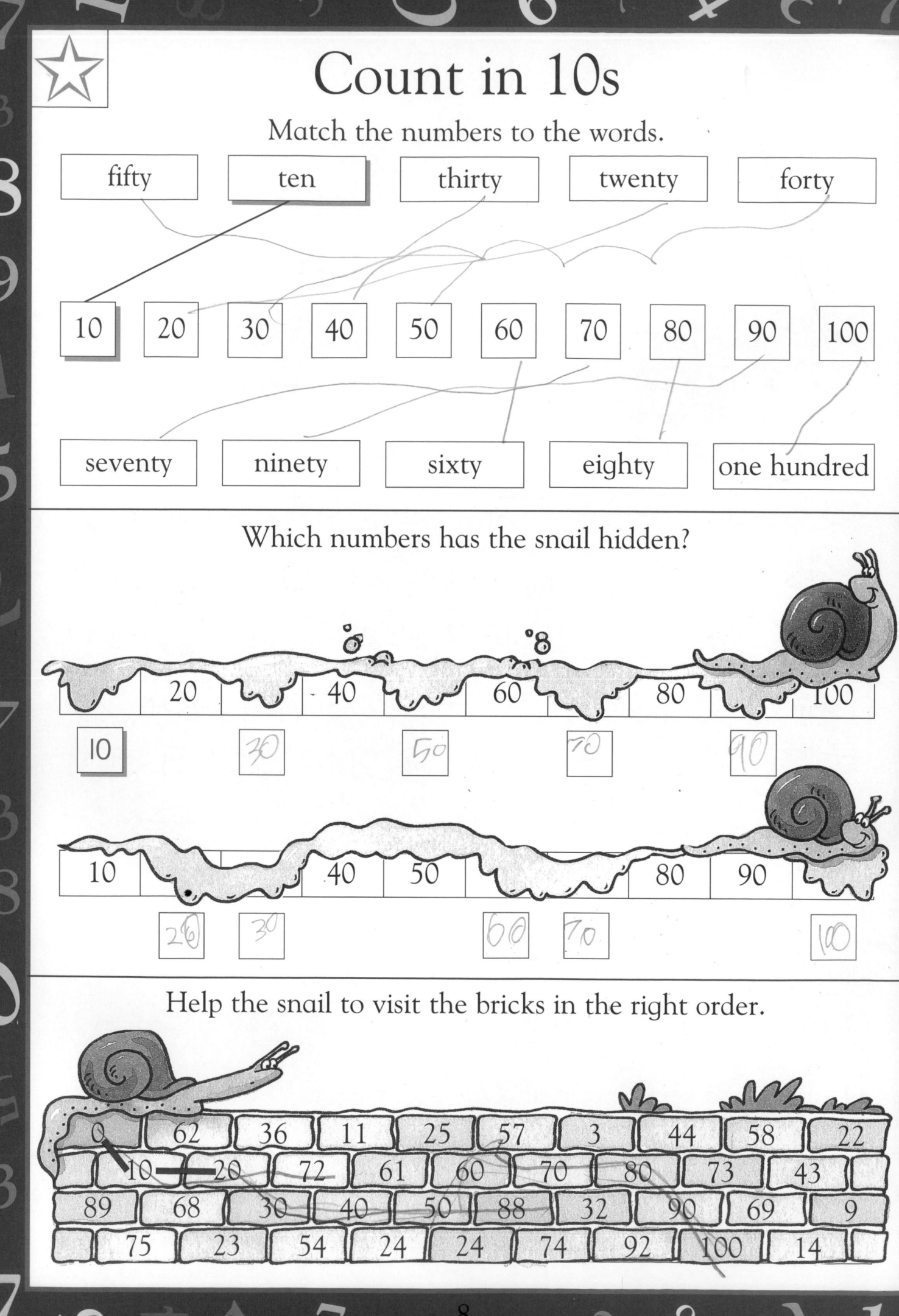

| | 20 | | 40 | | 60 | | 80 | | 100 |

| 10 | 30 | 50 | 70 | 90 |

| 10 | | | 40 | 50 | | | 80 | 90 | |

| 20 | 30 | | 60 | 70 | | 100 |

Help the snail to visit the bricks in the right order.

0	62	36	11	25	57	3	44	58	22
10	20	72	61	60	70	80	73	43	
89	68	30	40	50	88	32	90	69	9
75	23	54	24	24	74	92	100	14	

Count in 2s

Draw the 'hops' and circle the numbers.

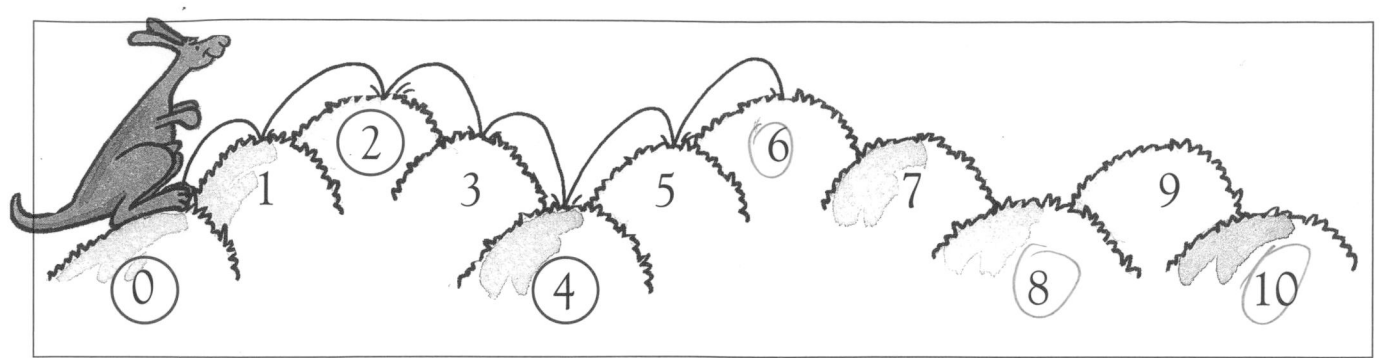

Colour the even numbers.

1	2	3	4	5
6	7	8	9	10
11	12	13	14	15
16	17	18	19	20
21	22	23	24	25
26	27	28	29	30

Join the dots in order.

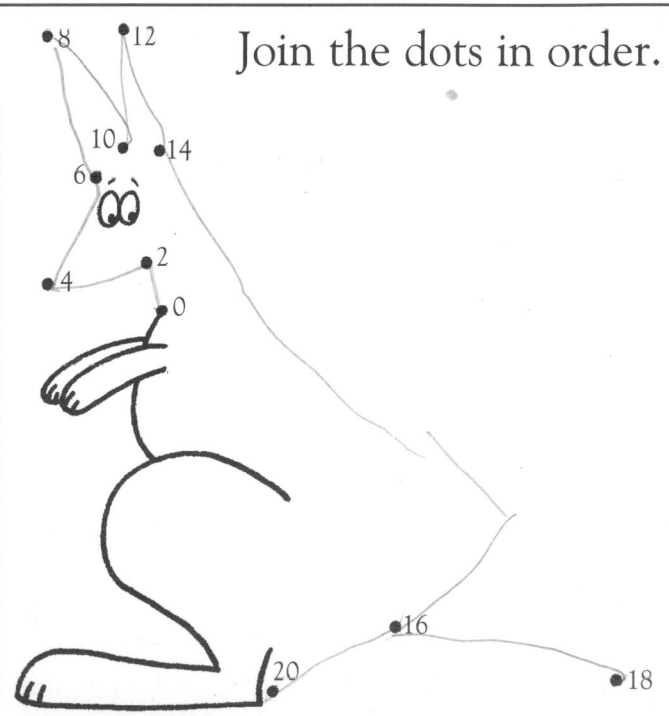

Patterns

Continue the pattern.

Make your own patterns.

Number patterns.

2	4	6	2	4	6	2	4	6	6	2	4	0
10	9	9	10	9	0	9	9	10	9	9	9	9
1	3	5	7	1	3	5	7	1	3	5	7	1
5	5	5	6	5	5	5	5	6	5	5	5	6

Number machines

Add the numbers and write the answers.

Machine +1 (left):
1 → 2
3 → 4
5 → 6
7 → 8
9 → 10

Machine +1 (right):
2 → 3
4 → 5
6 → 7
8 → 9
10 → 11

Machine +2 (left):
9 → 11
11 → 13
13 → 15
15 → 17
17 → 19

Machine +3 (right):
8 → 11
10 → 13
12 → 15
14 → 17
16 → 19

Machine +4 (left):
2 → 6
6 → 10
12 → 16
14 → 18
16 → 20

Machine +5 (right):
3 → 8
7 → 12
11 → 16
13 → 18
15 → 20

11

Reading numbers

Read the number and colour that many things.

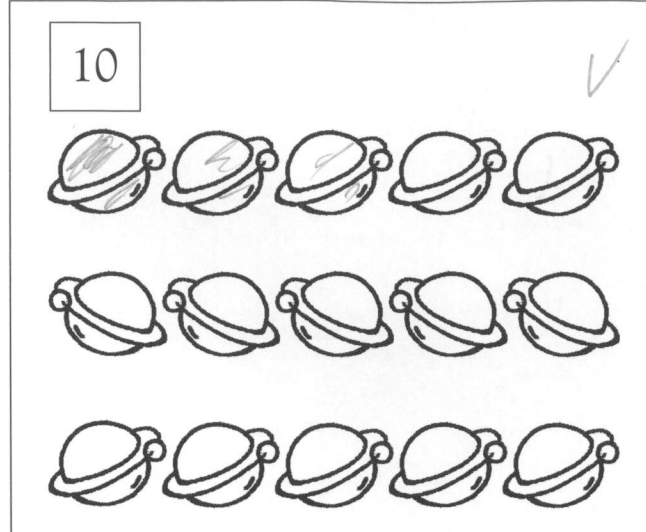

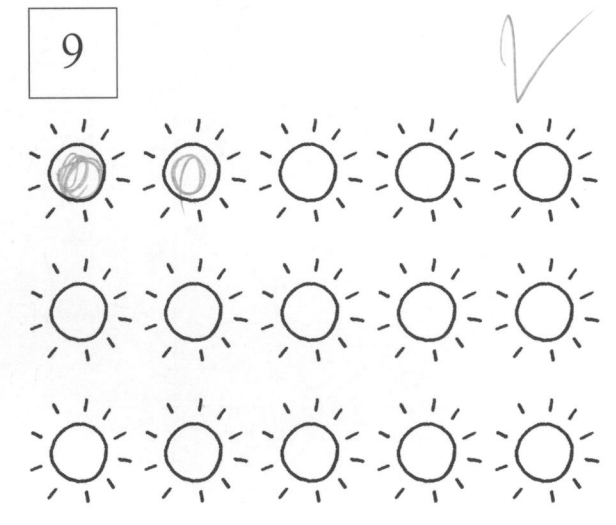

Draw your own example.

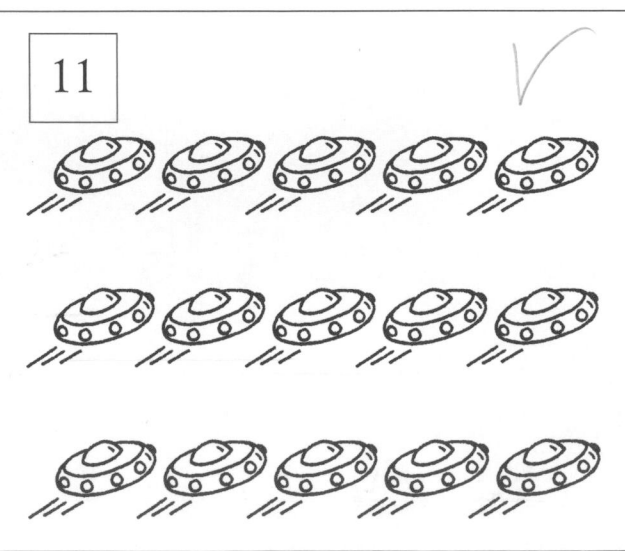

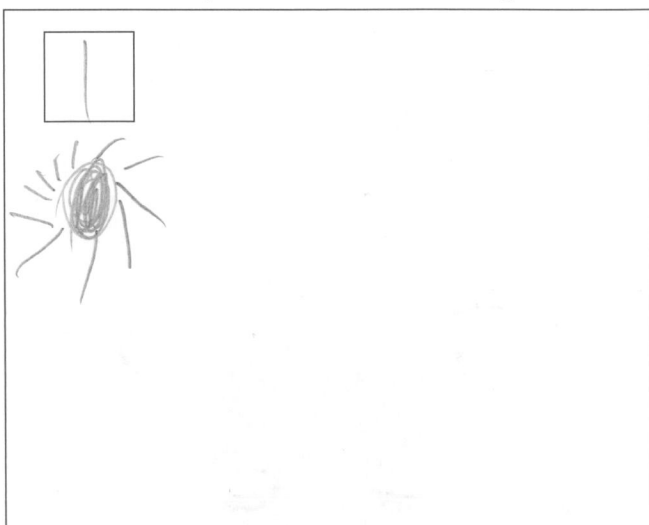

Ringing 10s

Ring around 10 and write the numbers.

12 ⟶ 10 and 2

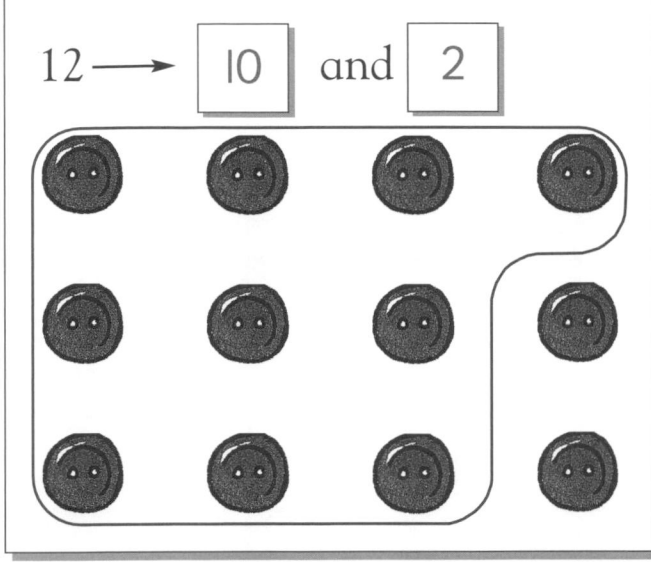

16 ⟶ 2 and 18

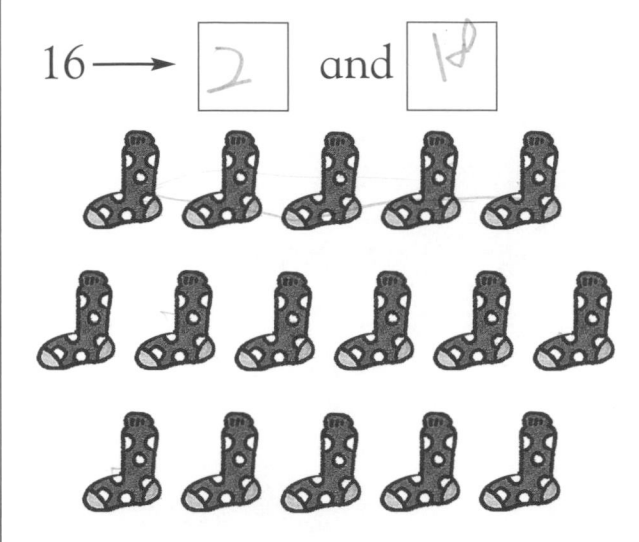

19 ⟶ 2 and 21

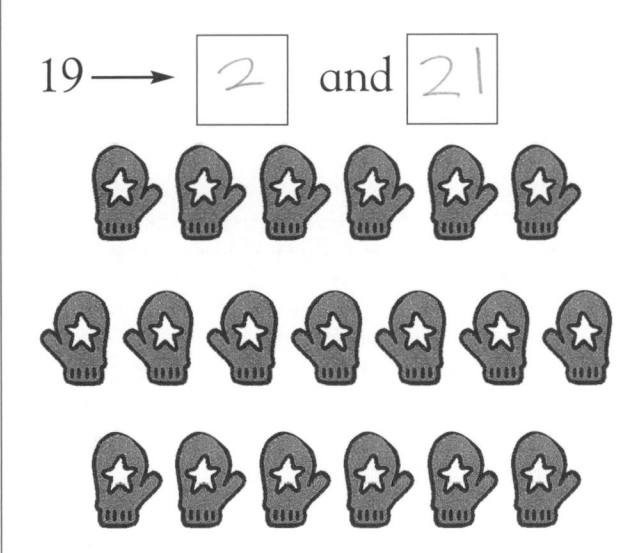

17 ⟶ 1 and 18

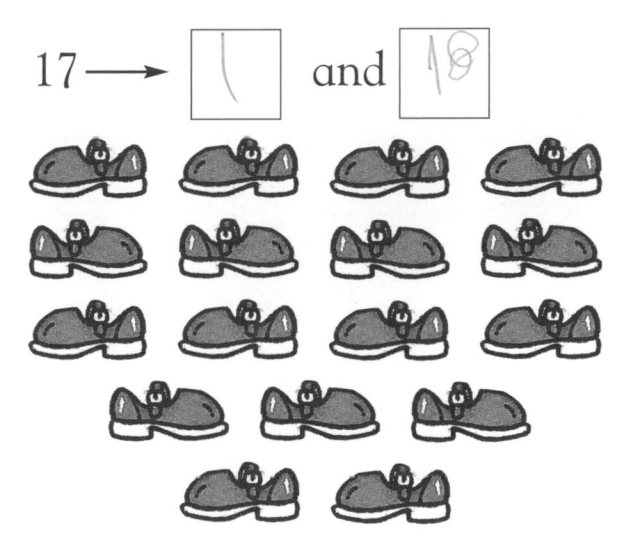

11 ⟶ 1 and 12

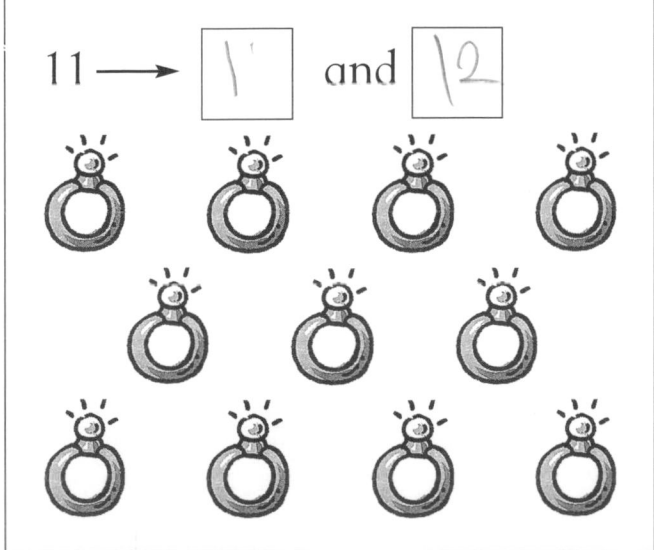

20 ⟶ 1 and 21

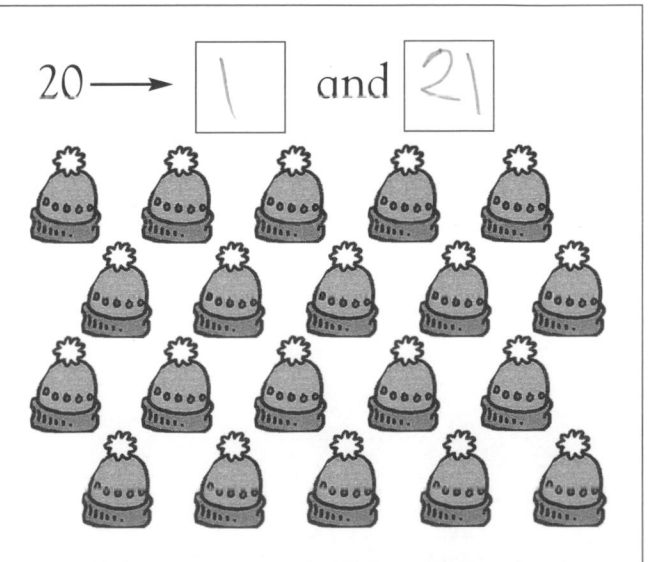

Tens and units

Write the tens and units.

tens	units	tens	units	tens	units
1	4	1	4	1	1

| 14 | | | | | |

Draw the tens and units.

tens	units	tens	units	tens	units
1	9	1	5	1	3

One more or one less?

Write one less and one more in the boxes.

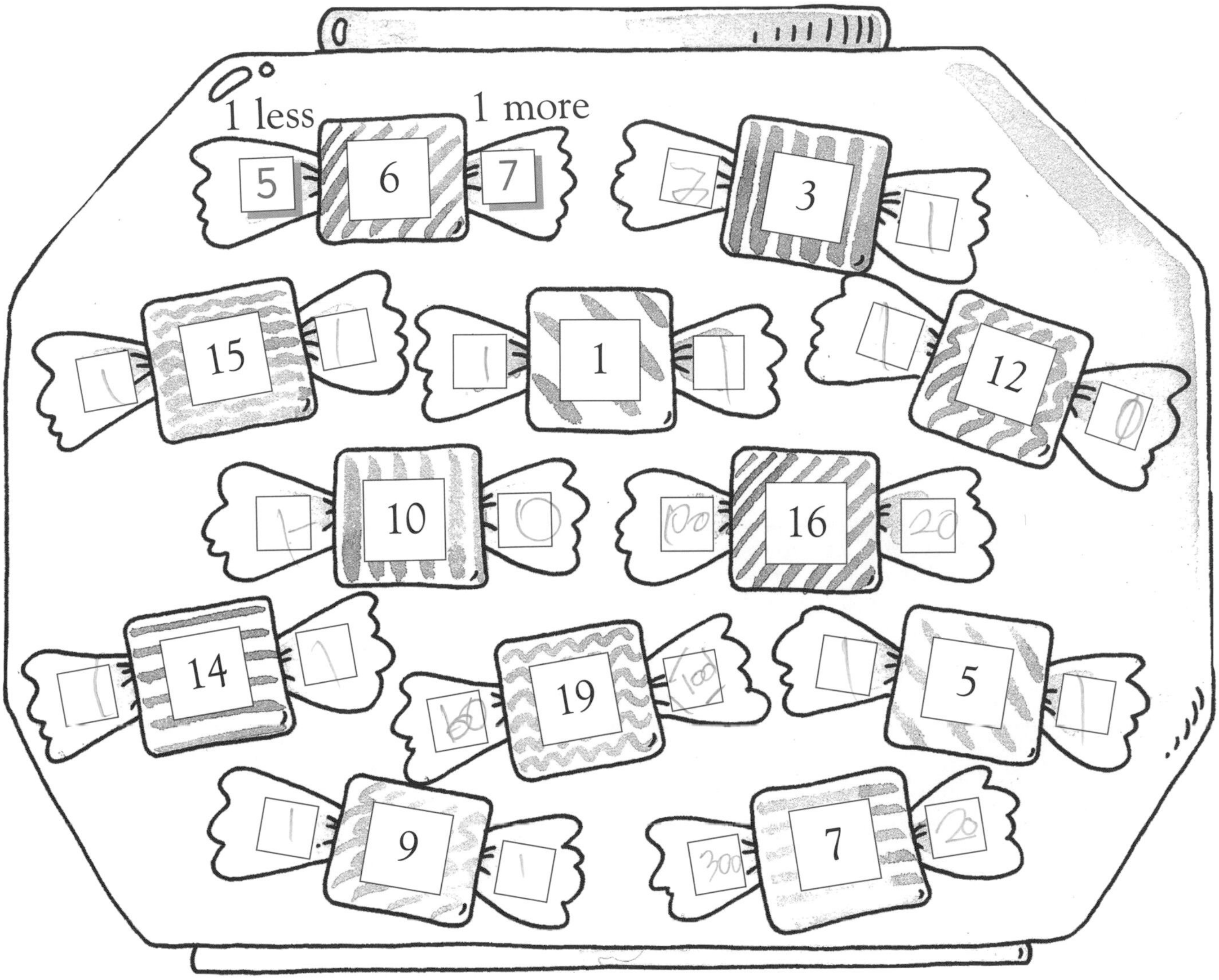

1 less   1 more

5 | 6 | 7

7 | 3 | 1

15 | 1 | 12

10 | 16

14 | 19 | 5

9 | 7

Draw one more or one less and write the number in the box.

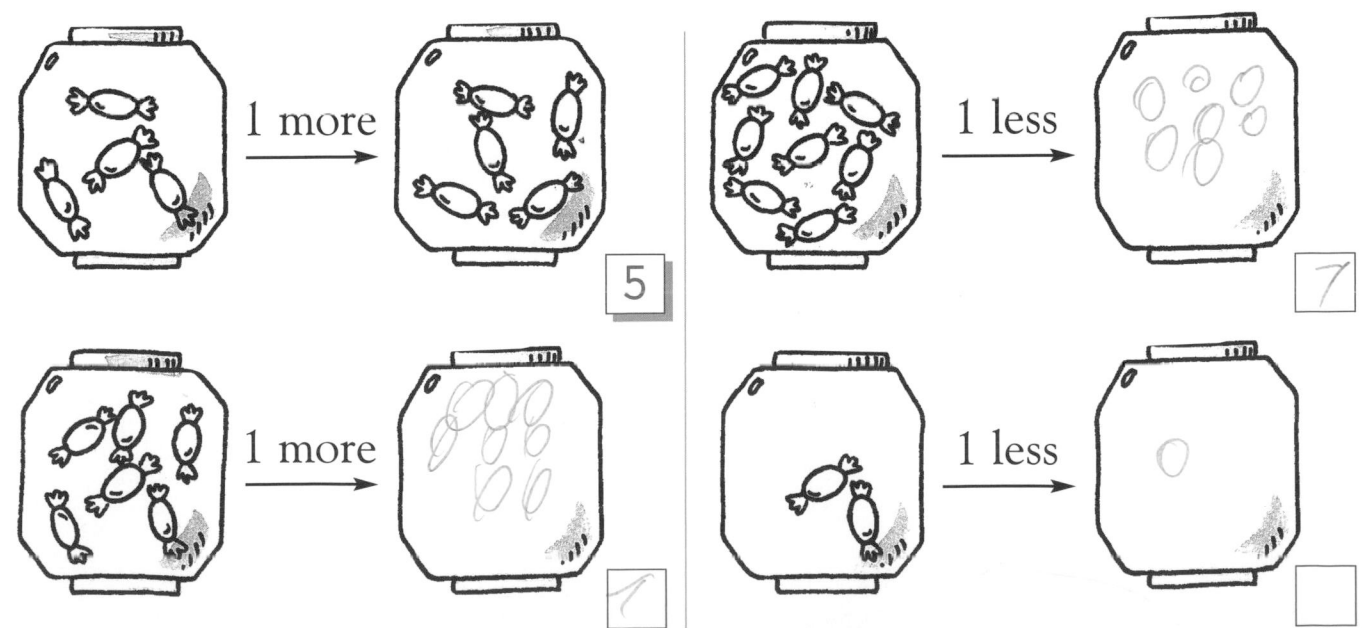

1 more →   5

1 less →   7

1 more →

1 less →

Ordering

Colour the rosettes.

4th = purple 3rd = yellow 1st = red 6th = green 2nd = blue 5th = orange

1st 2nd 3rd 4th 5th 6th

Write 1st, 2nd, 3rd ...

Write 1st, 2nd, 3rd ...

Start here

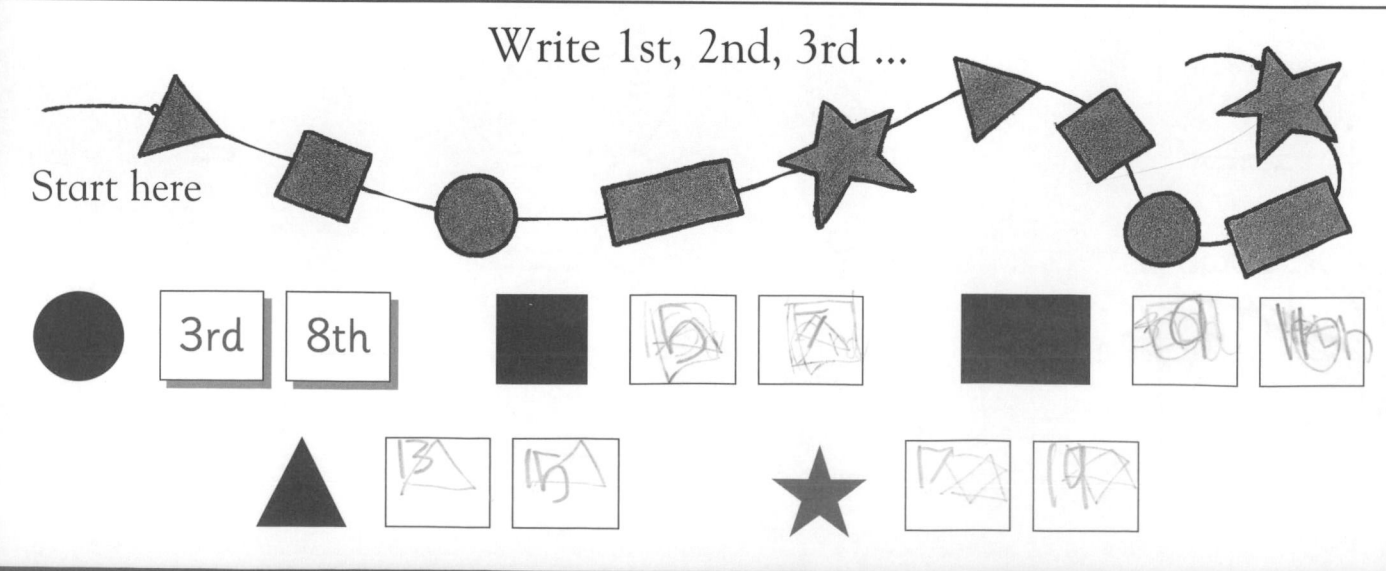

3rd 8th

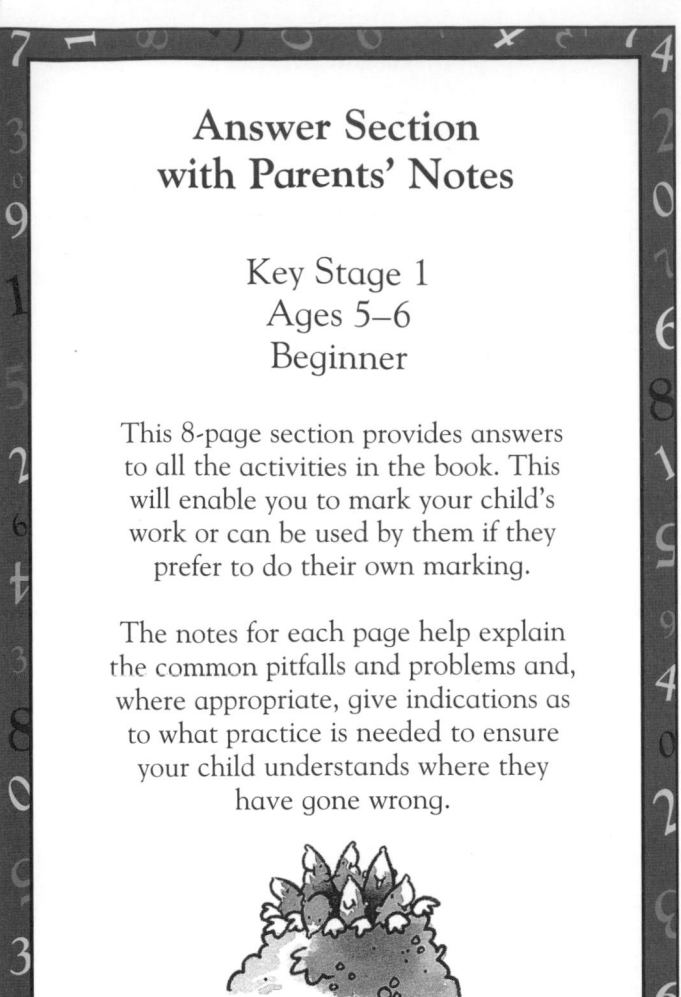

Answer Section with Parents' Notes

Key Stage 1
Ages 5–6
Beginner

This 8-page section provides answers to all the activities in the book. This will enable you to mark your child's work or can be used by them if they prefer to do their own marking.

The notes for each page help explain the common pitfalls and problems and, where appropriate, give indications as to what practice is needed to ensure your child understands where they have gone wrong.

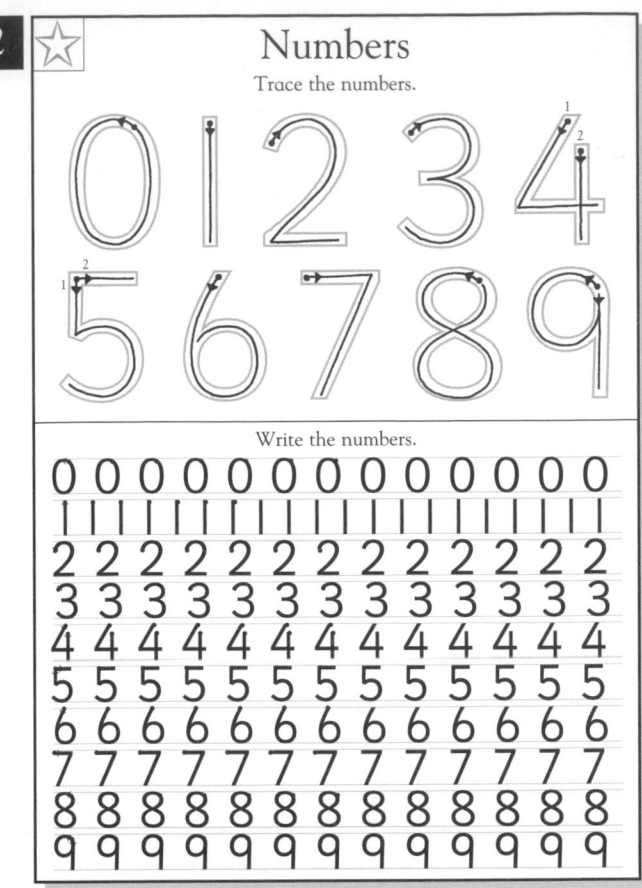

2

Numbers
Trace the numbers.

0 1 2 3 4
5 6 7 8 9

Write the numbers.

0 0 0 0 0 0 0 0 0 0 0 0 0
1 1 1 1 1 1 1 1 1 1 1 1 1
2 2 2 2 2 2 2 2 2 2 2 2 2
3 3 3 3 3 3 3 3 3 3 3 3 3
4 4 4 4 4 4 4 4 4 4 4 4 4
5 5 5 5 5 5 5 5 5 5 5 5 5
6 6 6 6 6 6 6 6 6 6 6 6 6
7 7 7 7 7 7 7 7 7 7 7 7 7
8 8 8 8 8 8 8 8 8 8 8 8 8
9 9 9 9 9 9 9 9 9 9 9 9 9

Correct formation of the digits is essential. Throughout Key Stage 1, children will need regular short doses of practice to reinforce the correct movement of the pencil. Watch out for reversed formation and for any digit written 'bottom-up'. All digits start from the top.

3

Numbers and pictures
Count the animals, draw the dots, and write the number.

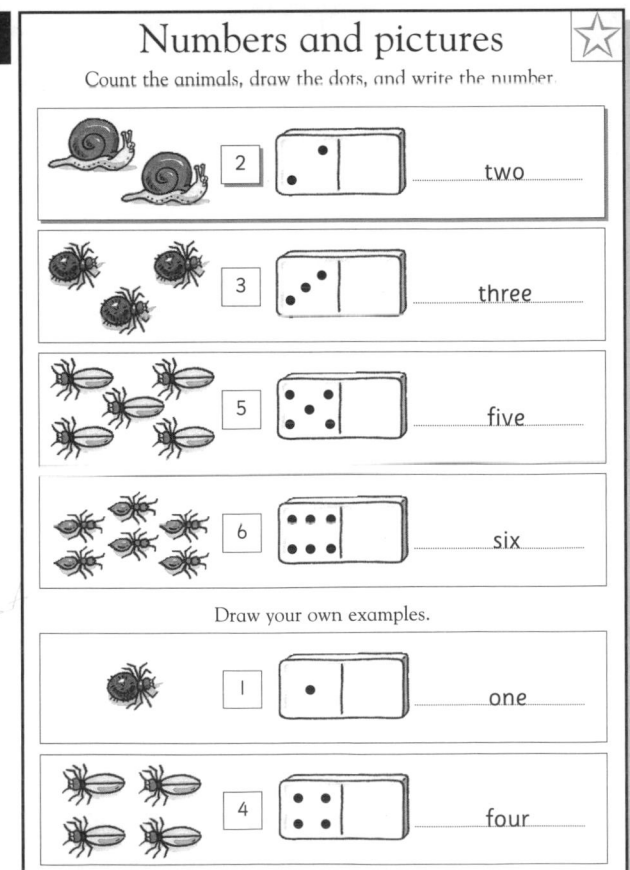

2	• •	two
3	• • •	three
5	• • • • •	five
6	• • • • • •	six

Draw your own examples.

| 1 | • | one |
| 4 | • • • • | four |

At this stage it is more important for the child to be able to read the word for each number than to be able to spell it without help. Correct spellings can be learned as the child is ready.

4

Counting
Join the set to the number.

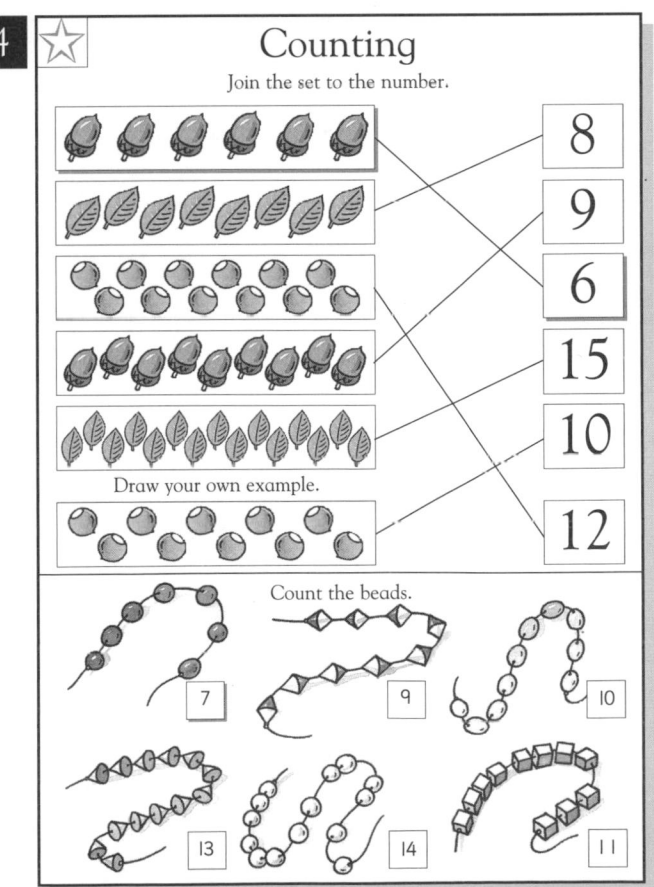

8
9
6
15
10
12

Draw your own example.

Count the beads.

7   9   10

13   14   11

Counting and then re-counting to check an answer is a useful habit to develop. Some children will be able to count by moving their eyes along the objects, but when re-counting, it will help the child to point to each thing as they count.

Counting out loud
Say and write the missing numbers.

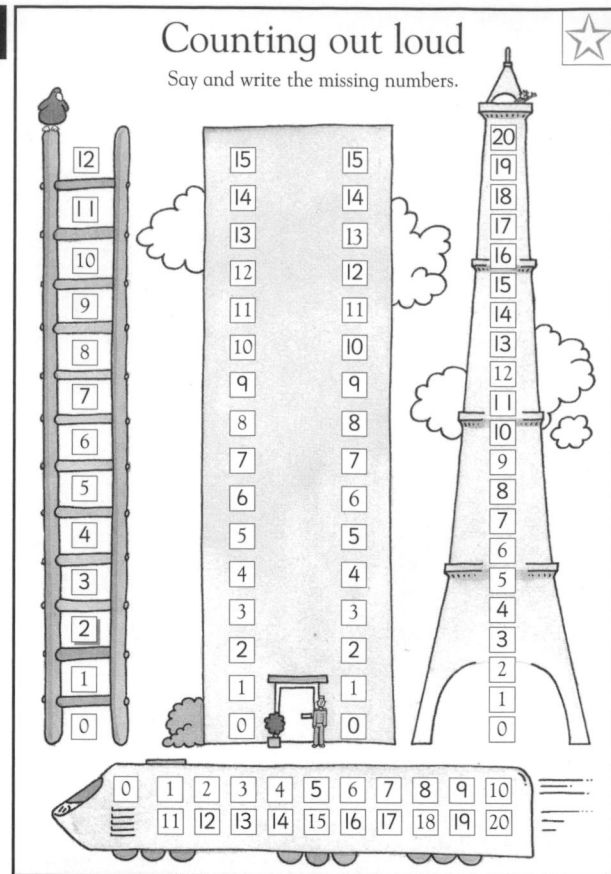

It is important that the child says the numbers out loud whilst completing each picture to reinforce the pattern of sounds that the numbers make. This will help them to get a feel for whether the sequence sounds right. Check that zero is understood here.

Missing numbers
Write in the missing numbers.

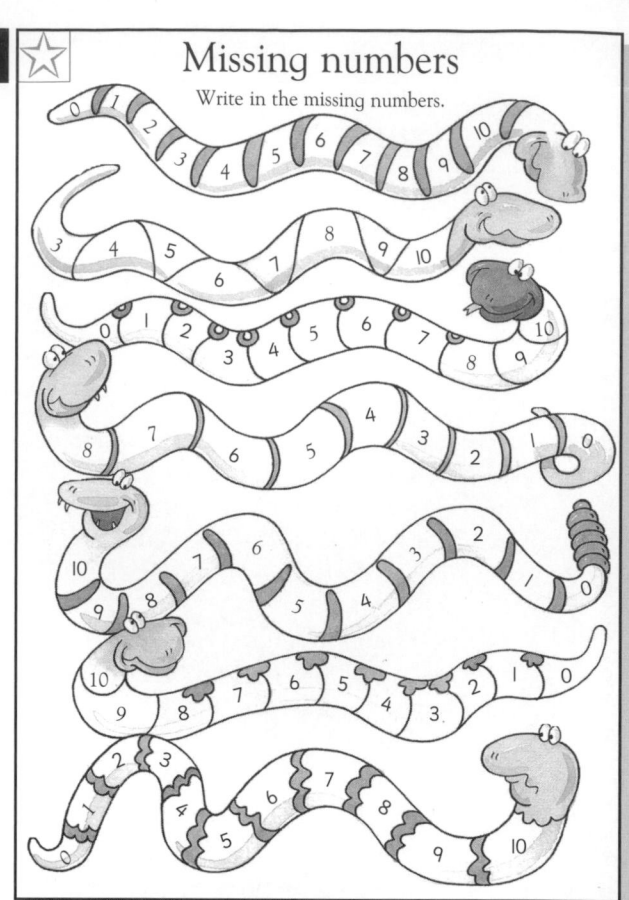

On snakes 4 and 6 watch that the child writes 0 (zero) as the number nearest the tail and not 1. It is essential to encourage the use of the term 'zero' and not 'nought', 'O' (as in 'only'), or 'nothing'.

Number bonds
Colour some of the fish red, and write the numbers in the boxes.

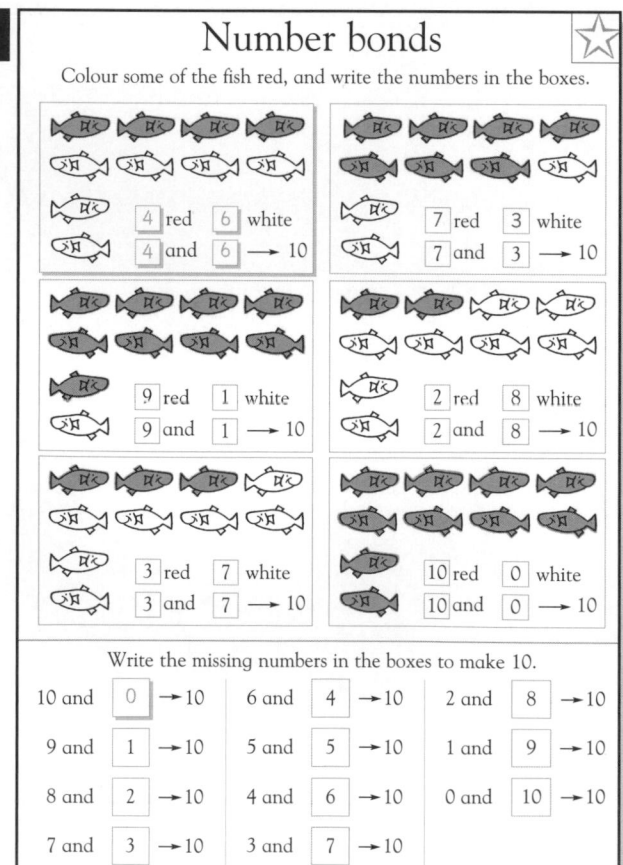

It is important that the number of items coloured matches the number written in the answer boxes. In the bottom activity, find out whether the child has noticed the pattern as it is developing. Learning these pairs of numbers (number bonds) will help later on.

Count in 10s
Match the numbers to the words.

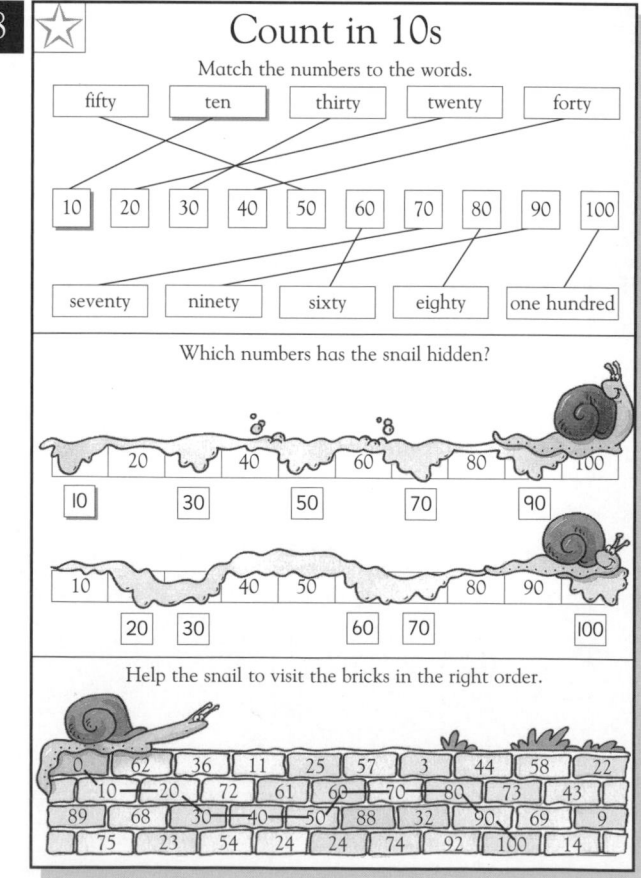

Can the child recite the sequence and then do it in reverse from 100 back down to 10? Point out that all of the number words except the 'ten' and the 'hundred' end in '-ty'. They also begin with the same two letters as their unit number (e.g. thirty and three).

Count in 2s
Draw the 'hops' and circle the numbers.

Encourage the child to read out loud the sequence of numbers they have found: '2, 4, 6, 8'. In the grid activity (bottom left) make sure the child notices the pattern emerging and understands that the coloured squares are 'even' and the others are 'odd' numbers.

Patterns
Continue the pattern.

Make your own patterns.

Number patterns.

Encourage the child to talk about their own patterns and to explain what they have done. You could explain that, to be a mathematical pattern, something must repeat in a predictable way. There is more than one way for the last patterns to be repeated.

Number machines
Add the numbers and write the answers.

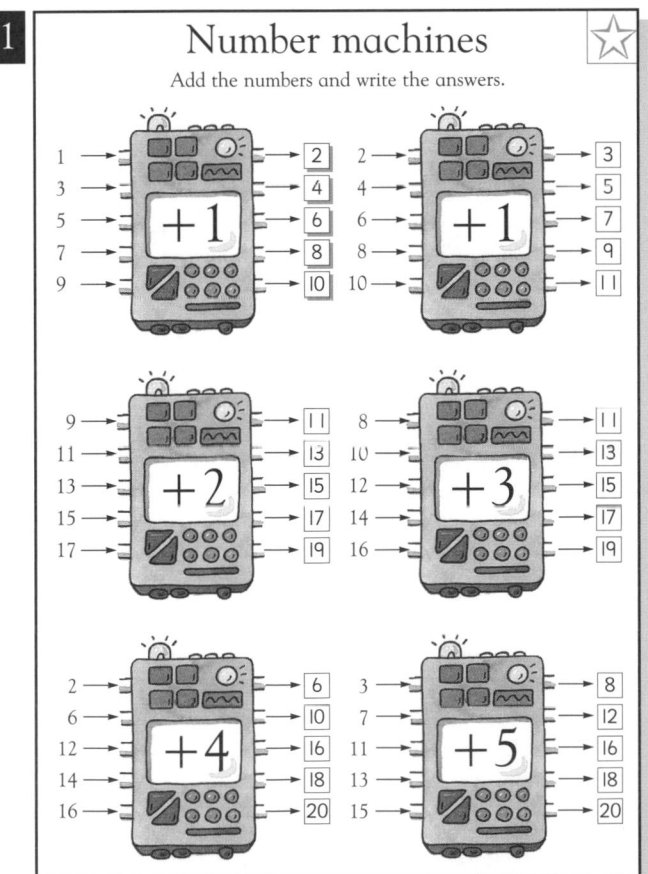

Has the child noticed the pattern of numbers? Explain that if the numbers are going up in steps of one, then the answers go up in steps of one, too. Similarly, if the numbers are going up in twos, then the answers go up in twos as well.

Reading numbers
Read the number and colour that many things.

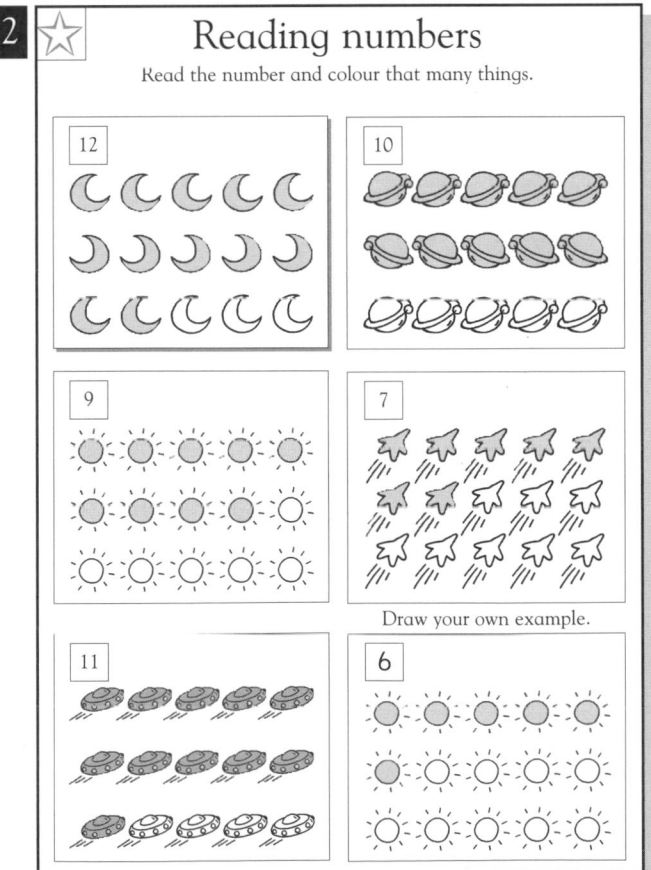

Draw your own example.

When checking how many pictures the child has coloured, encourage them to go back and re-count '1, 2, 3 ...' out loud each time. It will help if the child points to each picture as they count it. Help the child to count systematically.

Ringing 10s
Ring around 10 and write the numbers.

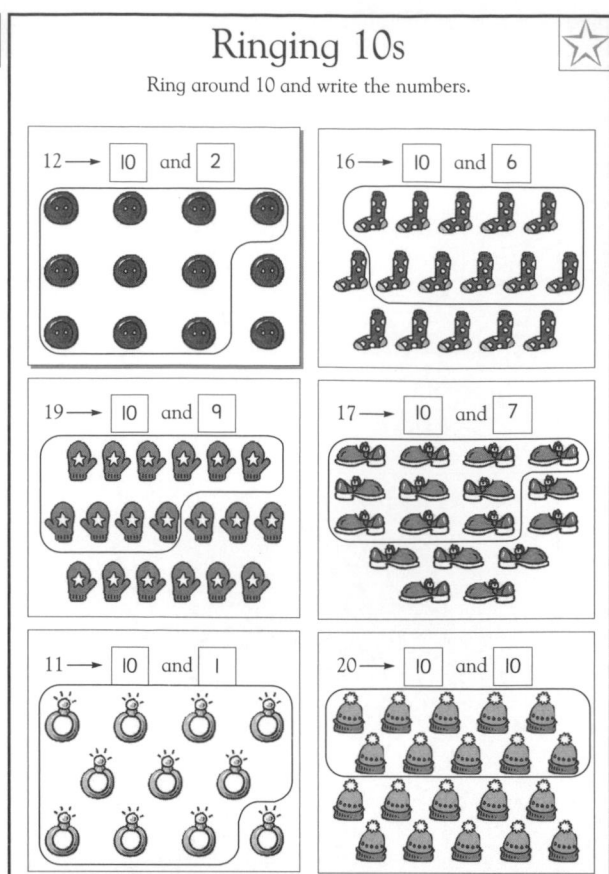

Before marking the number sentences, check that each drawn ring does actually enclose 10 objects. A miscount here will affect the numbers counted outside and will give an incorrect result.

Tens and units
Write the tens and units.

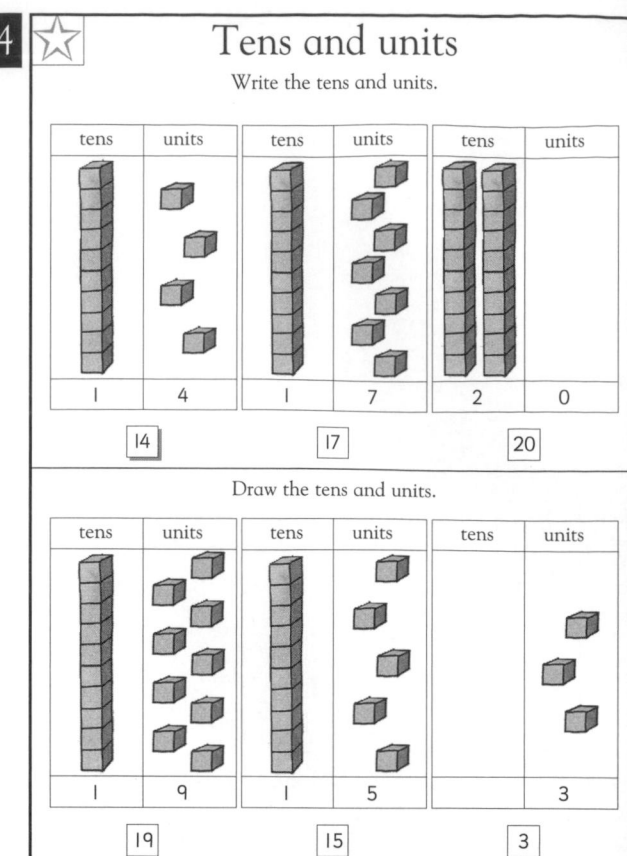

Continue to draw attention to the way the ten numbers are written. Check that the child can tell you that the 1 in 14 is 'worth' ten but the 1 in 41 or in 1 is only worth one single one or unit.

One more or one less?
Write one less and one more in the boxes.

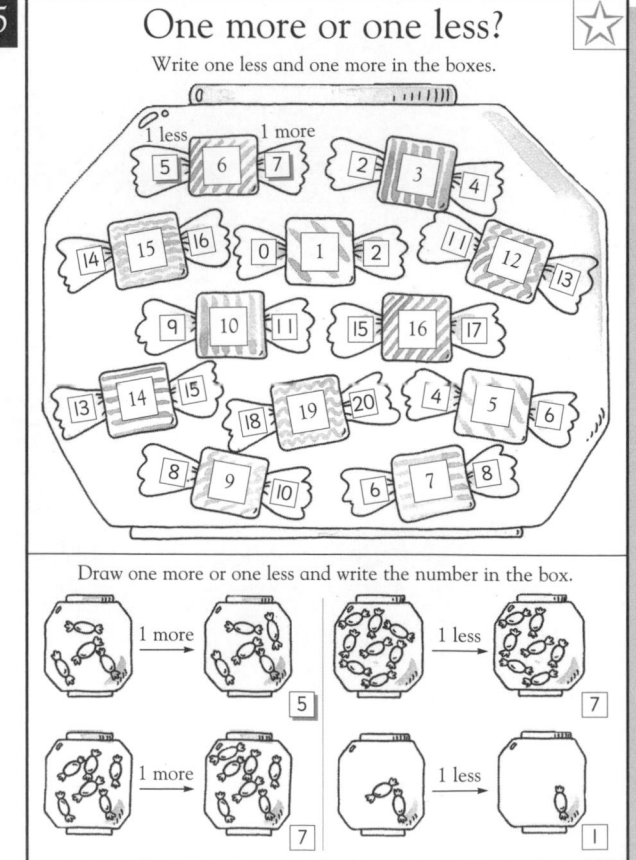

Understanding will be further increased if the child is helped to make up their own number stories about the sweets. For example, Rebecca had 3 sweets already, but her Mum said she had been so good she could have 1 more. Rebecca has 4 sweets now.

Ordering
Colour the rosettes.

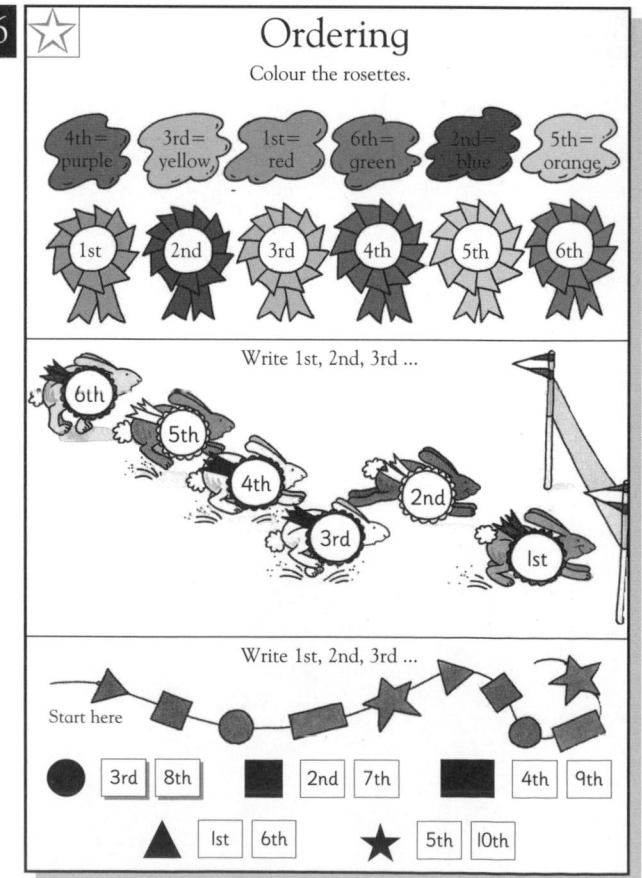

Check that the child really does see the relationship between the numbers and the ordinals e.g. position 3 is 3rd and position 10 is 10th etc. They should then be able to tell you what the last place would be in a race with any number of animals.

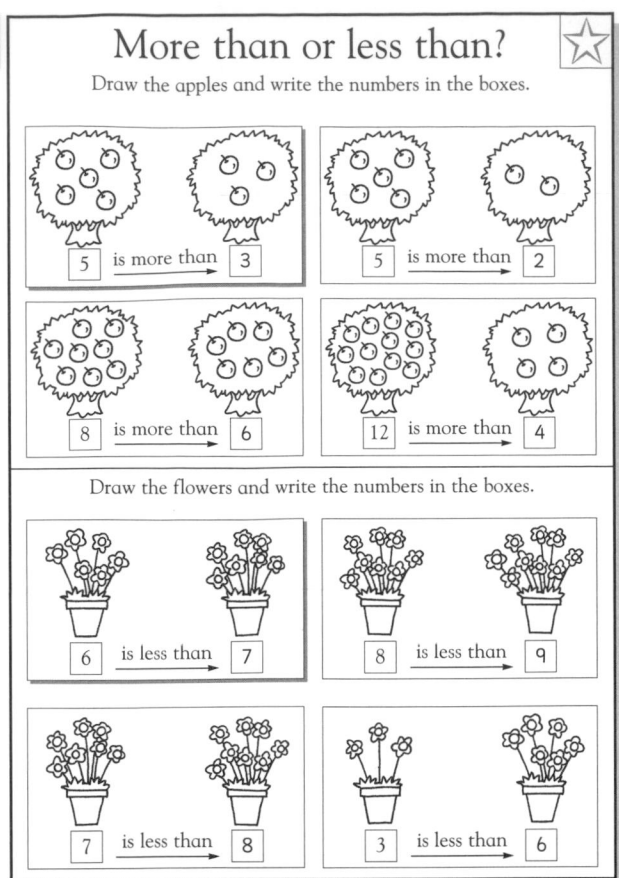

17

More than or less than?
Draw the apples and write the numbers in the boxes.

5 is more than 3
5 is more than 2
8 is more than 6
12 is more than 4

Draw the flowers and write the numbers in the boxes.

6 is less than 7
8 is less than 9
7 is less than 8
3 is less than 6

Several variations on the above are possible. In the top activity, the child should have drawn apples and written a number to match the number drawn e.g. 5, 4 ,3, 2, 1 or 0 apples. In the bottom activity, the number should match the number of flowers drawn.

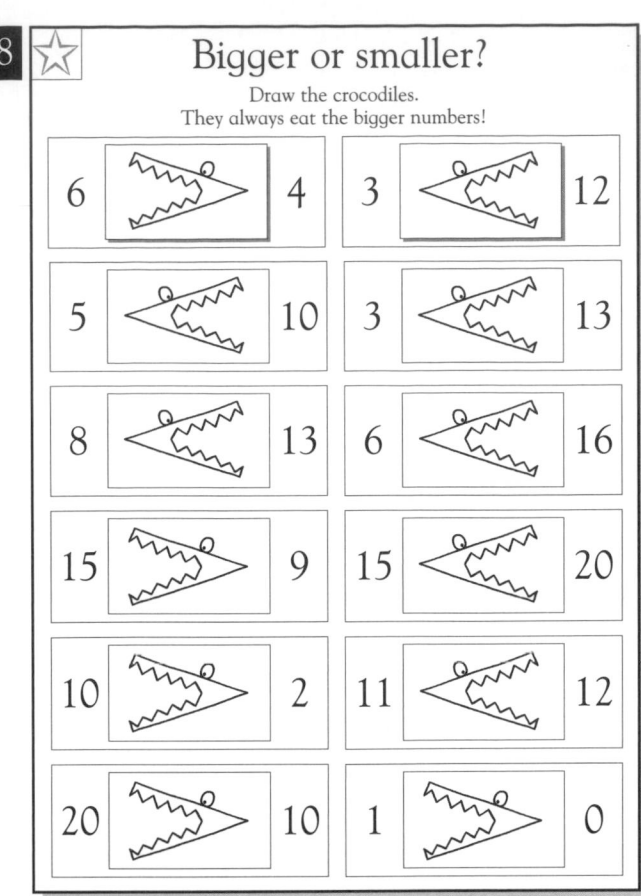

18

Bigger or smaller?
Draw the crocodiles.
They always eat the bigger numbers!

6	4	3	12
5	10	3	13
8	13	6	16
15	9	15	20
10	2	11	12
20	10	1	0

It is important to check that the child understands the word 'bigger' as being different to 'big'. They may see 1 as a very small number and therefore the last question may be confusing. Confirming that yes, one is small, but it is still bigger than zero will help.

19

Comparing

heavier   lighter   bigger smaller   longer   shorter

Draw the pictures and say ...

heavier than → heavier than
lighter than → lighter than
bigger than → bigger than
smaller than → smaller than
longer than → longer than
shorter than → shorter than

If the child experiences difficulty in comparing three objects, let them try actually holding pairs of household objects. Encourage them to compare these side by side and to get used to using the language involved before moving back onto sets of three objects.

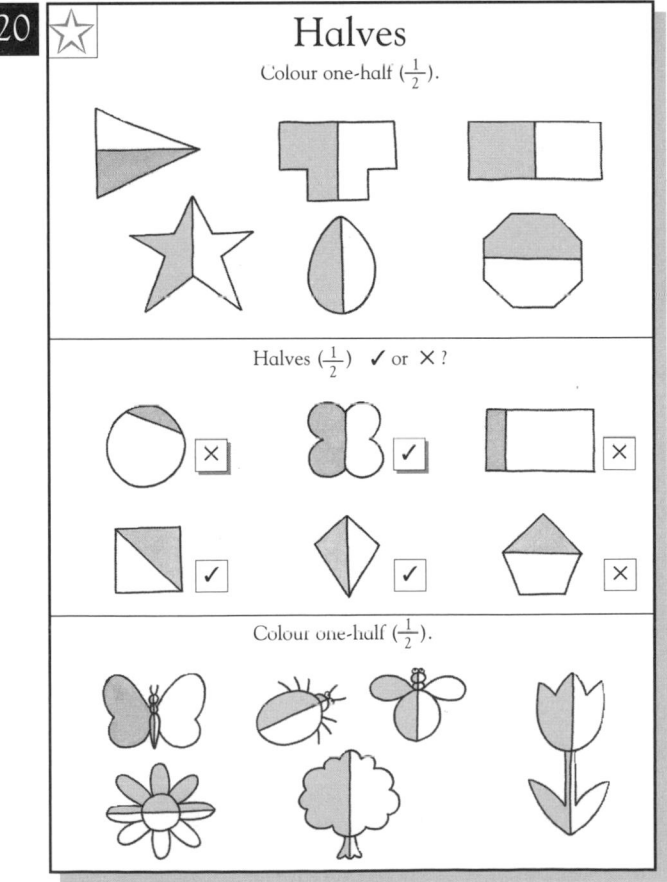

20

Halves
Colour one-half ($\frac{1}{2}$).

Halves ($\frac{1}{2}$) ✓ or ✗ ?

| ✗ | ✓ | ✗ |
| ✓ | ✓ | ✗ |

Colour one-half ($\frac{1}{2}$).

The word 'half' is frequently misused to simply mean one of two 'bits'. It is vital to ensure the child appreciates that the two pieces must be of identical size. It may help to cut out paper shapes and to fold them along the line of symmetry.

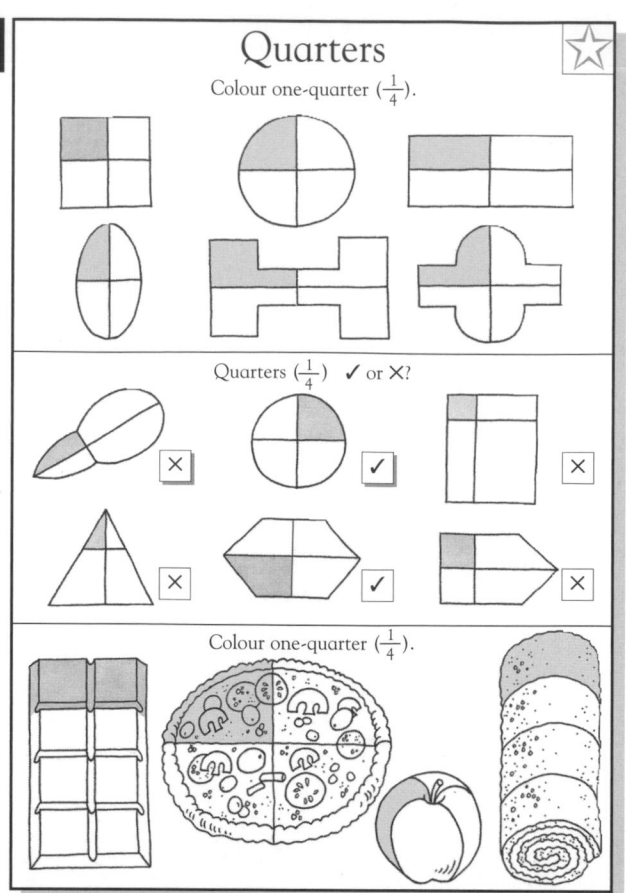

21 Quarters

Colour one-quarter ($\frac{1}{4}$).

Quarters ($\frac{1}{4}$) ✓ or ✗?

✗ ✓ ✗
✗ ✓ ✗

Colour one-quarter ($\frac{1}{4}$).

The child should be able to explain that 'four quarters', means four parts of equal size and that if the parts are not equal then they are not quarters. Some children will not make the connection automatically between four parts and the way one-quarter is written.

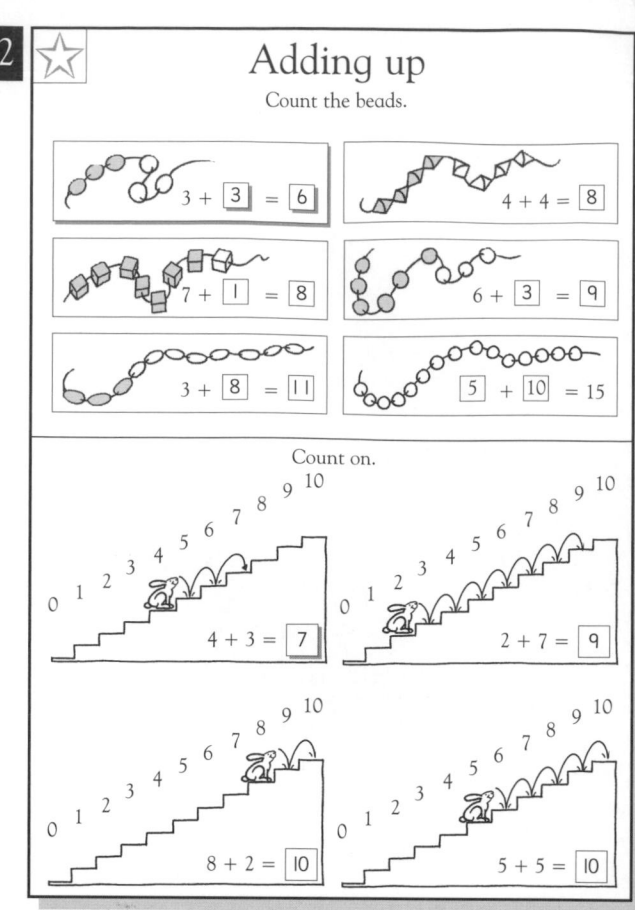

22 Adding up

Count the beads.

$3 + \boxed{3} = \boxed{6}$ $4 + 4 = \boxed{8}$

$7 + \boxed{1} = \boxed{8}$ $6 + \boxed{3} = \boxed{9}$

$3 + \boxed{8} = \boxed{11}$ $\boxed{5} + \boxed{10} = 15$

Count on.

$4 + 3 = \boxed{7}$ $2 + 7 = \boxed{9}$

$8 + 2 = \boxed{10}$ $5 + 5 = \boxed{10}$

In the final example in the top activity, any one of a number of combinations would be correct but the two numbers written must match the two numbers of bead coloured. In the second activity, encourage mental calculation by asking the child to count in their head.

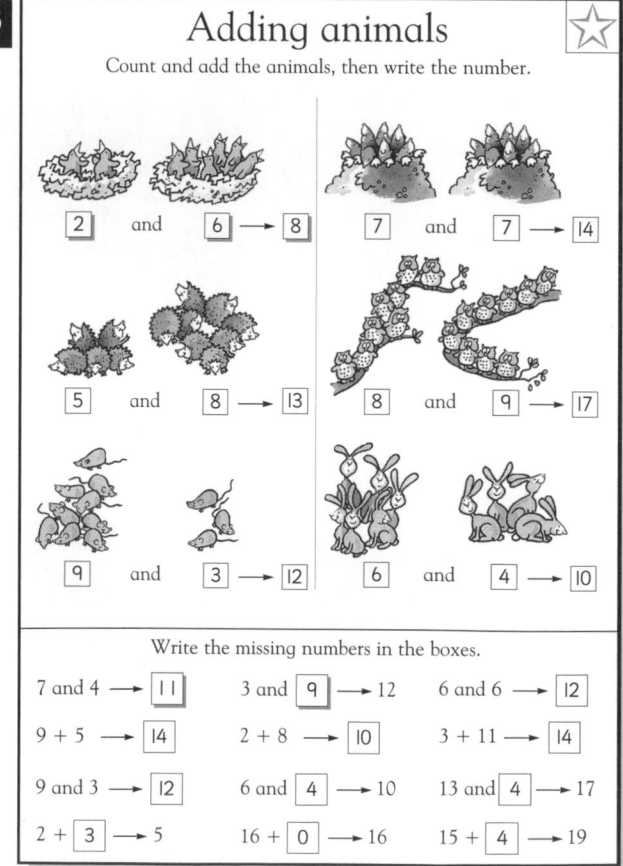

23 Adding animals

Count and add the animals, then write the number.

$\boxed{2}$ and $\boxed{6}$ → $\boxed{8}$ $\boxed{7}$ and $\boxed{7}$ → $\boxed{14}$

$\boxed{5}$ and $\boxed{8}$ → $\boxed{13}$ $\boxed{8}$ and $\boxed{9}$ → $\boxed{17}$

$\boxed{9}$ and $\boxed{3}$ → $\boxed{12}$ $\boxed{6}$ and $\boxed{4}$ → $\boxed{10}$

Write the missing numbers in the boxes.

7 and 4 → $\boxed{11}$ 3 and $\boxed{9}$ → 12   6 and 6 → $\boxed{12}$

9 + 5 → $\boxed{14}$ 2 + 8 → $\boxed{10}$ 3 + 11 → $\boxed{14}$

9 and 3 → $\boxed{12}$ 6 and $\boxed{4}$ → 10   13 and $\boxed{4}$ → 17

2 + $\boxed{3}$ → 5   16 + $\boxed{0}$ → 16   15 + $\boxed{4}$ → 19

Encourage children to develop good habits by counting on to work out the answers here.

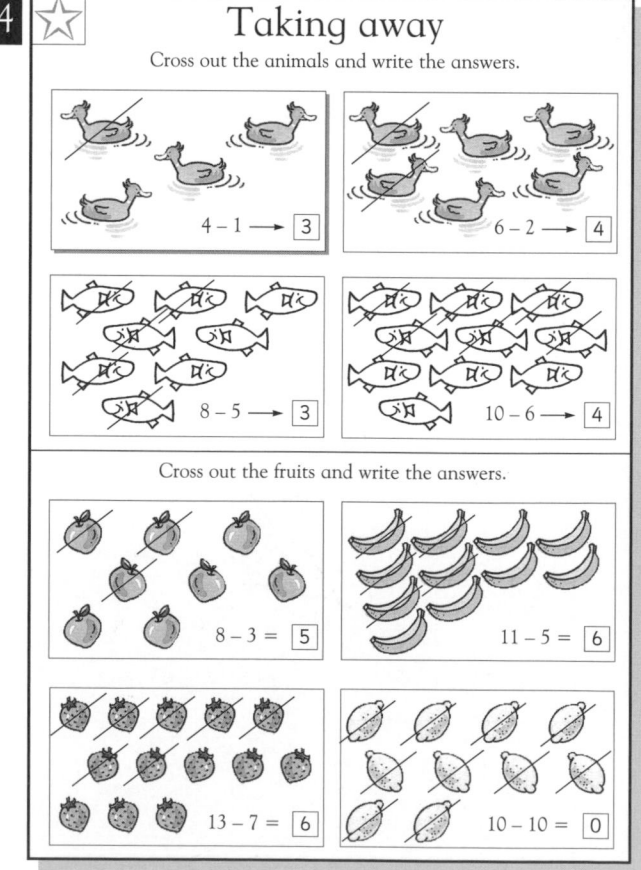

24 Taking away

Cross out the animals and write the answers.

$4 - 1$ → $\boxed{3}$ $6 - 2$ → $\boxed{4}$

$8 - 5$ → $\boxed{3}$ $10 - 6$ → $\boxed{4}$

Cross out the fruits and write the answers.

$8 - 3 = \boxed{5}$ $11 - 5 = \boxed{6}$

$13 - 7 = \boxed{6}$ $10 - 10 = \boxed{0}$

Ask the child to talk about what they have done and to use the terms 'crossing out' and 'leaves behind'. They may already know 'take away' and it would be useful for them to see that crossing out is a way of taking away the pictures.

Counting back

Count back.

$9 - 3 = \boxed{6}$

$5 - 1 = \boxed{4}$

$8 - 2 = \boxed{6}$

$7 - 0 = \boxed{7}$

$3 - 3 = \boxed{0}$

$10 - 8 = \boxed{2}$

Write the missing numbers in the boxes.

$3 - 3 = \boxed{0}$ $20 - 10 = \boxed{10}$ $9 - \boxed{3} = 6$ $15 - \boxed{10} = 5$

$5 - 4 = \boxed{1}$ $8 - 8 = \boxed{0}$ $5 - \boxed{5} = 0$ $20 - \boxed{16} = 4$

$15 - 4 = \boxed{11}$ $19 - 9 = \boxed{10}$ $6 - \boxed{4} = 2$ $18 - \boxed{7} = 11$

$10 - 9 = \boxed{1}$ $16 - 9 = \boxed{7}$ $13 - \boxed{3} = 10$ $10 - \boxed{6} = 4$

Encourage the child to use mental calculation with the smaller numbers. Putting the bigger number 'in your head' before counting back is often successful.

Lots of

Write the missing numbers in the boxes.

$\boxed{2}$ lots of $\boxed{3}$ ⟶ $\boxed{6}$

$\boxed{2}$ lots of $\boxed{5}$ ⟶ $\boxed{10}$

$\boxed{3}$ lots of $\boxed{4}$ ⟶ $\boxed{12}$

$\boxed{3}$ lots of $\boxed{2}$ ⟶ $\boxed{6}$

$\boxed{4}$ lots of $\boxed{2}$ ⟶ $\boxed{8}$

Draw your own pictures in the boxes.

$\boxed{3}$ lots of $\boxed{3}$ ⟶ $\boxed{9}$

$\boxed{2}$ lots of $\boxed{4}$ ⟶ $\boxed{8}$

It is important to talk about the pictures and what they are showing. If the answers are wrong, check that the child hasn't simply added the two numbers, e.g. 2 lots of 3 added together to make 5.

Money

Which coin?

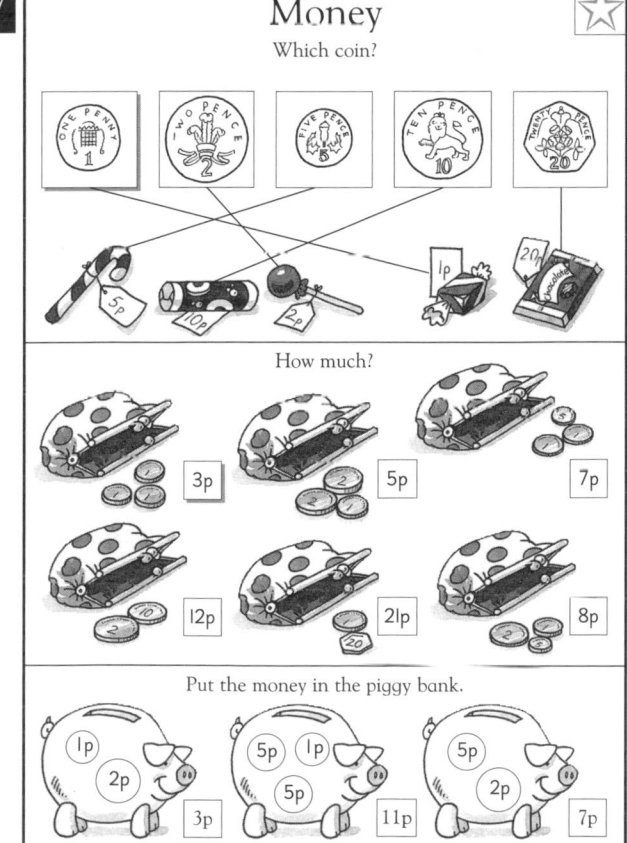

How much?

3p   5p   7p

12p   21p   8p

Put the money in the piggy bank.

3p   11p   7p

In the last activity, a number of combinations would be correct and it is important to re-count these with the child when marking. e.g. (1p 1p 1p 1p 1p 1p 1p), (2p 2p 2p 1p), (2p 1p 1p 1p 1p 1p), or (5p 2p). Explain that it is easier to use fewer coins where possible.

Ordering stories

Write 1st, 2nd, or 3rd.

2nd   3rd   1st

3rd   1st   2nd

3rd   2nd   1st

1st   2nd   3rd

Draw a line to 1st, 2nd, 3rd, or 4th.

4th   2nd   1st   3rd

Even more important than the order chosen by the child will be their reasons for so choosing and their ability to discuss these. It will help to relate the pictures to events in the child's own day and to the order in which things happen.

Time

Write the times in the boxes.

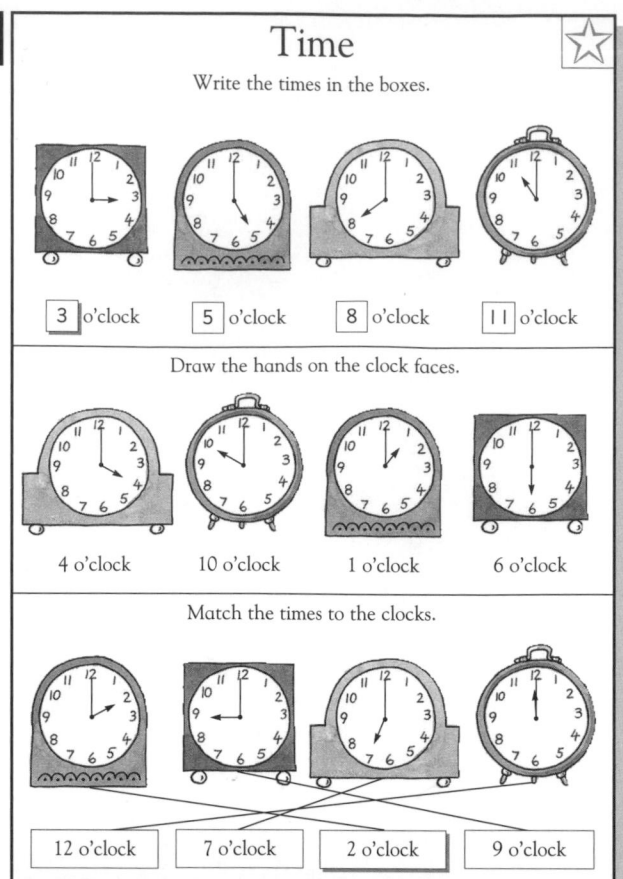

3 o'clock   5 o'clock   8 o'clock   11 o'clock

Draw the hands on the clock faces.

4 o'clock   10 o'clock   1 o'clock   6 o'clock

Match the times to the clocks.

12 o'clock   7 o'clock   2 o'clock   9 o'clock

Ask the child what they notice about the minute (big) hand on all of these clocks. They need to see and to talk about the fact that it always points to twelve when it is something o'clock. Count around the numbers from 1 to 12 with the child if necessary.

Graphs

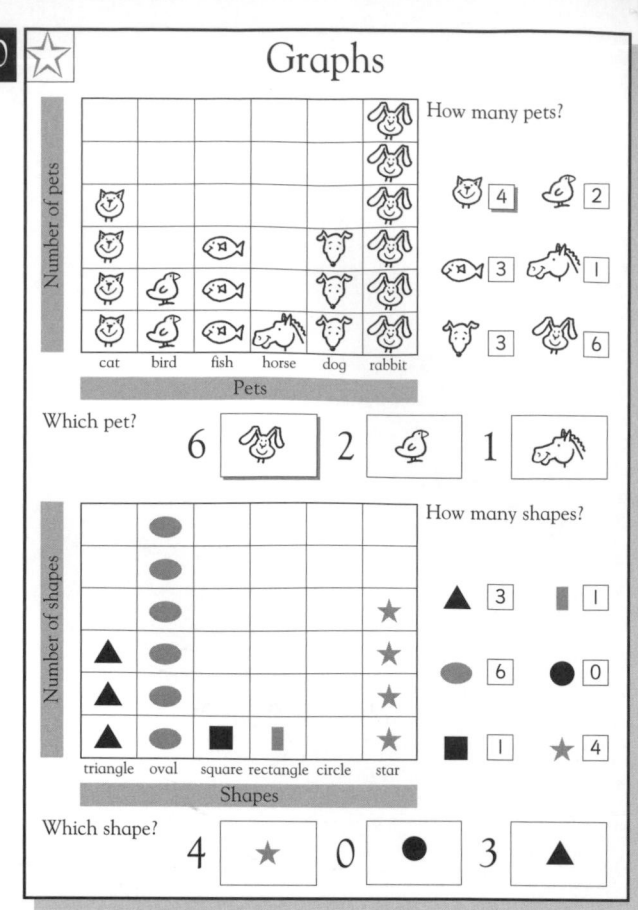

How many pets?

cat   bird   fish   horse   dog   rabbit

Pets

Number of pets

Which pet?   6   2   1

How many shapes?

triangle   oval   square   rectangle   circle   star

Shapes

Number of shapes

Which shape?   4 ★   0 ●   3 ▲

Before tackling the questions, encourage the child to talk about the graph and all that it shows. What is the highest number? (6). How many different types of pets are there across the graph? (6).

2D shapes

= yellow   = green   = purple   = blue

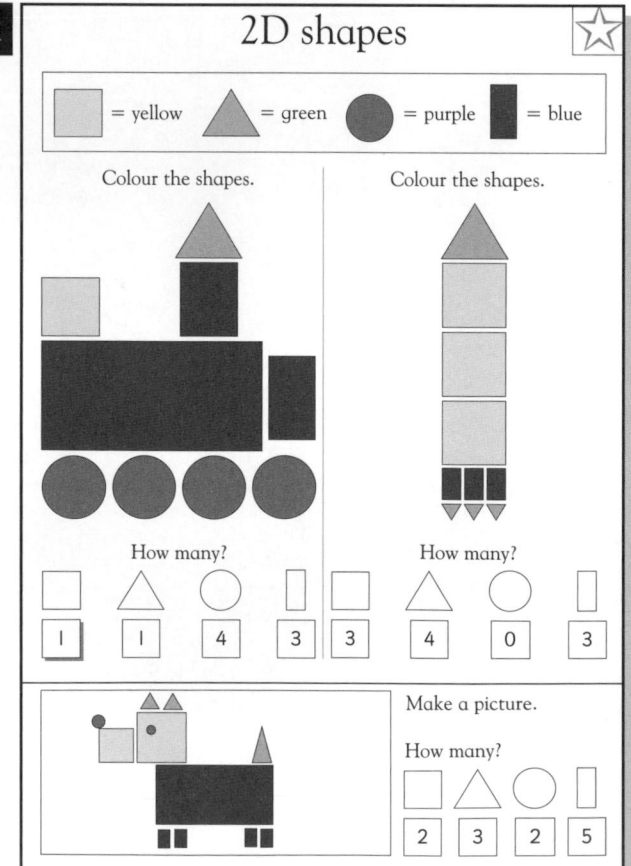

Colour the shapes.   Colour the shapes.

How many?   How many?

1   1   4   3   3   4   0   3

Make a picture.

How many?

2   3   2   5

In the last activity, talk to the child about their own picture, encouraging them to name each shape used. Ask them to re-count the shapes with you when checking how many of each one they have used.

3D shapes

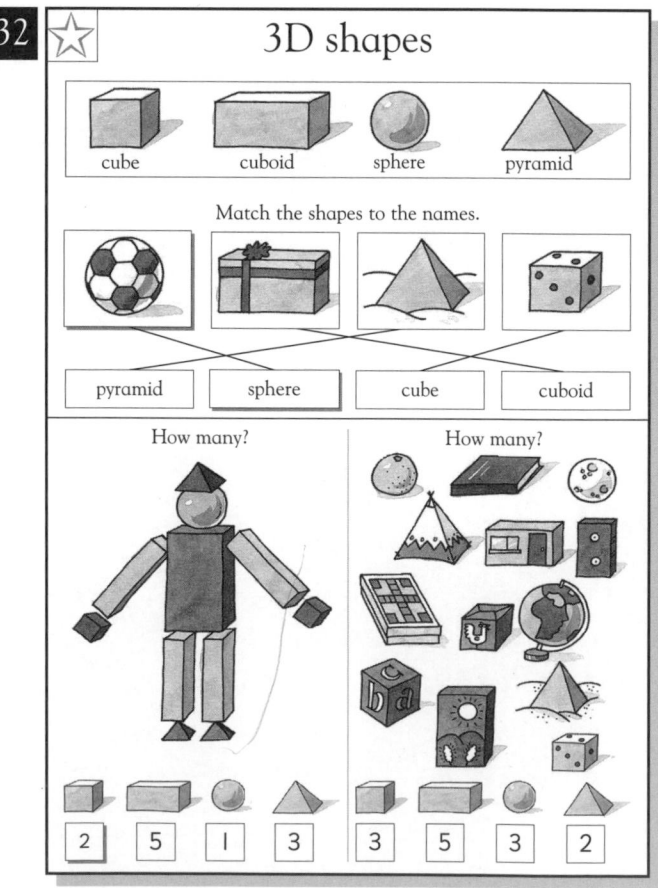

cube   cuboid   sphere   pyramid

Match the shapes to the names.

pyramid   sphere   cube   cuboid

How many?   How many?

2   5   1   3   3   5   3   2

Can the child hunt around their toy box or a food cupboard to find real-life examples of these shapes? Check that they recognise the same shapes positioned differently. For instance, do they recognise a pyramid standing on its point?

More than or less than?

Draw the apples and write the numbers in the boxes.

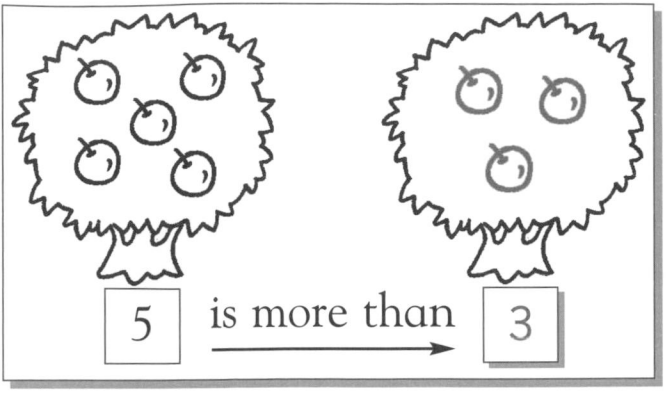

| 5 | is more than → | 3 |

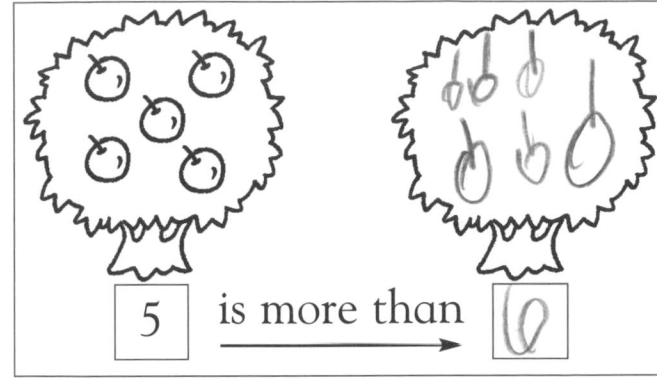

| 5 | is more than → | 6 |

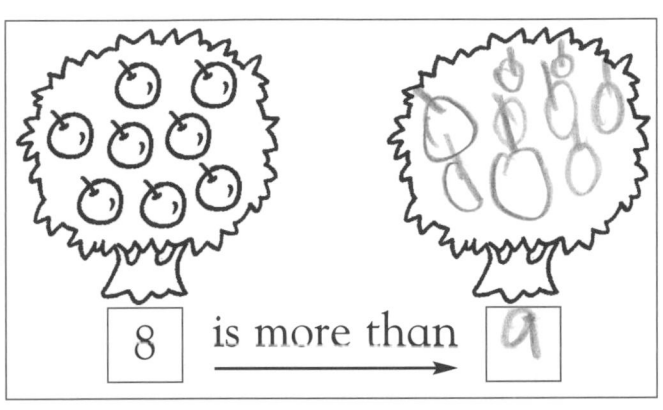

| 8 | is more than → | 9 |

| 12 | is more than → | 13 |

Draw the flowers and write the numbers in the boxes.

| 6 | is less than → | 7 |

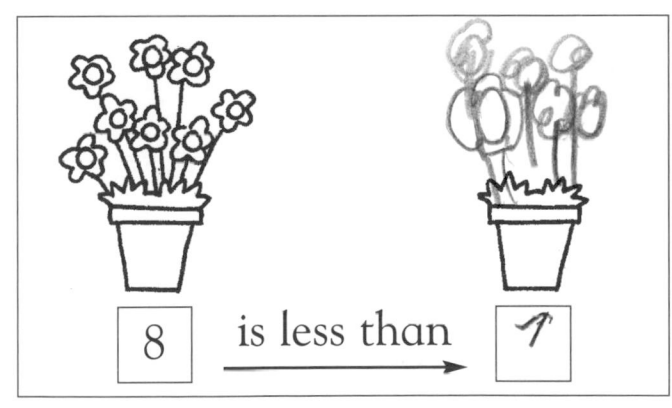

| 8 | is less than → | 7 |

| 7 | is less than → | 0 |

| 3 | is less than → | 2 |

Bigger or smaller?

Draw the crocodiles.
They always eat the bigger numbers!

6 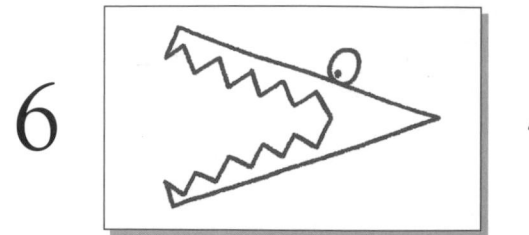 4

3 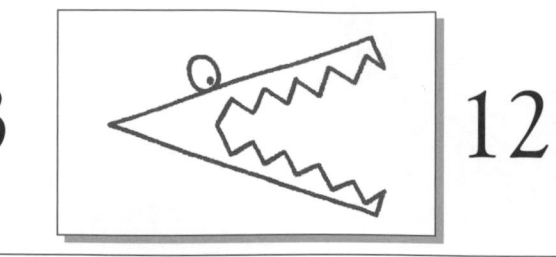 12

5 10

3  13

8 13

6  16

15 9

15  20

10 2

11  12

20 10

1 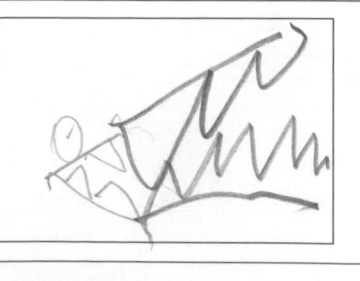 0

Comparing

heavier lighter bigger smaller longer shorter

Draw the pictures and say ...

		heavier than		heavier than	

		lighter than		lighter than	

		bigger than		bigger than	

		smaller than		smaller than	

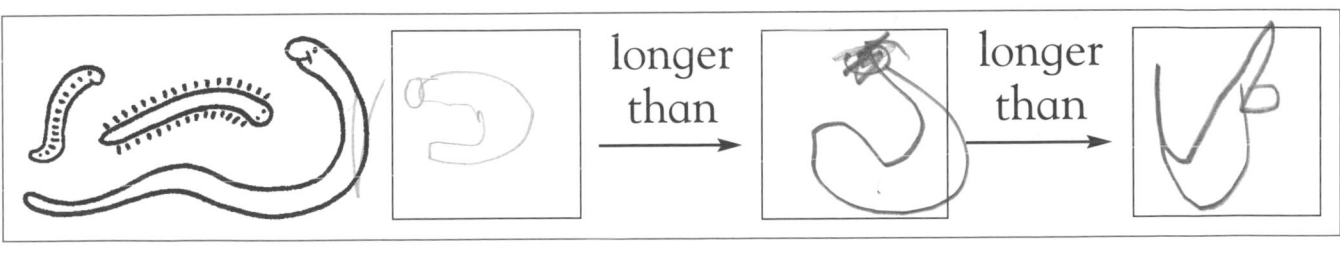

		longer than		longer than	

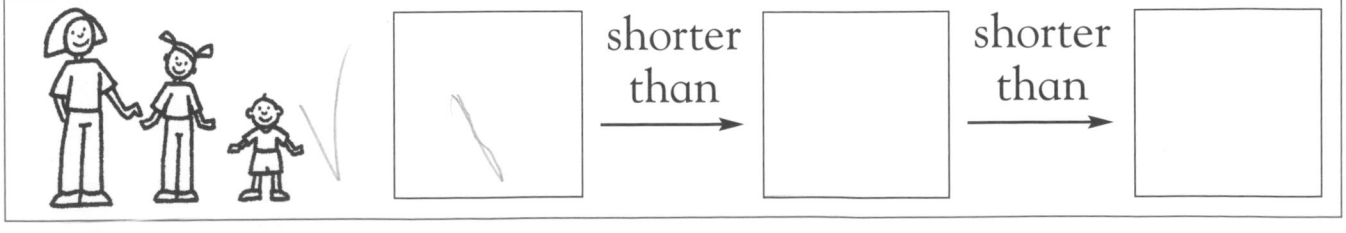

		shorter than		shorter than	

Halves

Colour one-half ($\frac{1}{2}$).

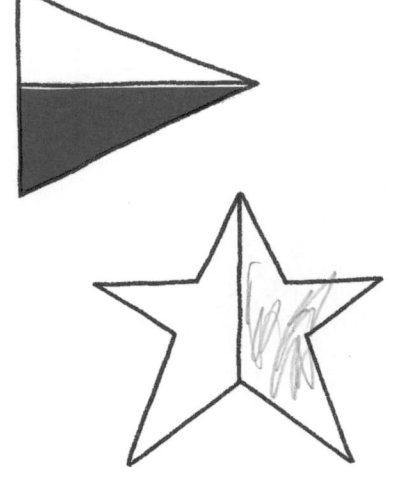 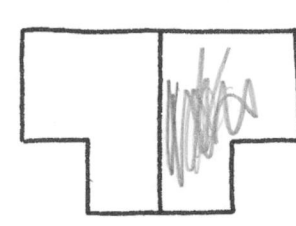 

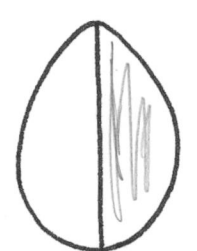 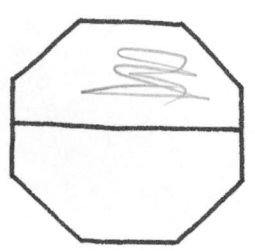

Halves ($\frac{1}{2}$) ✔ or ✗?

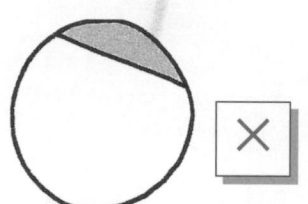  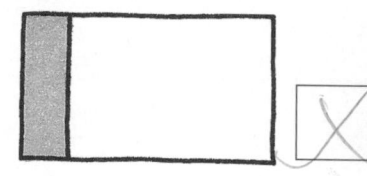

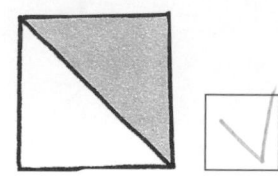 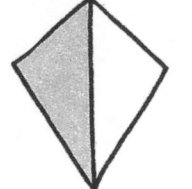 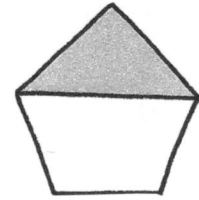 

Colour one-half ($\frac{1}{2}$).

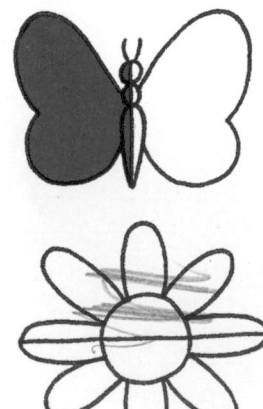   

Quarters

Colour one-quarter ($\frac{1}{4}$).

 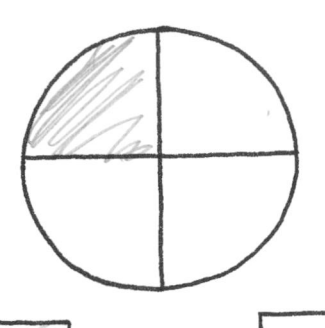 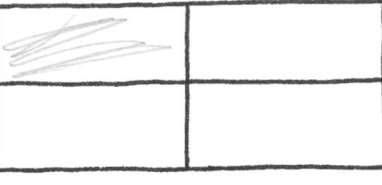

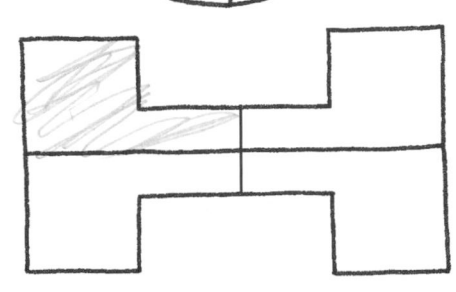 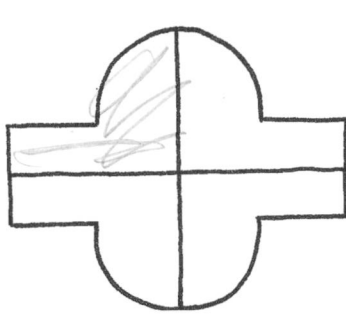

Quarters ($\frac{1}{4}$) ✓ or ✗?

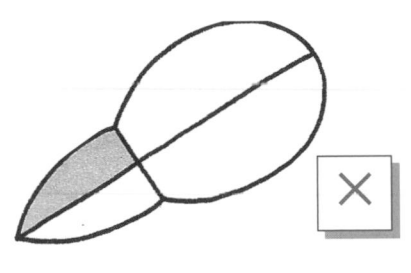 ✗

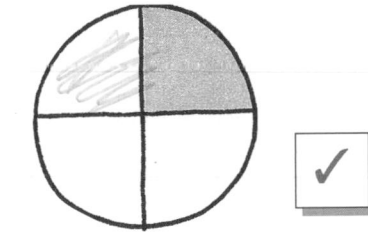 ✓

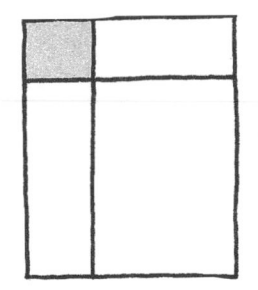 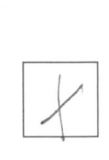

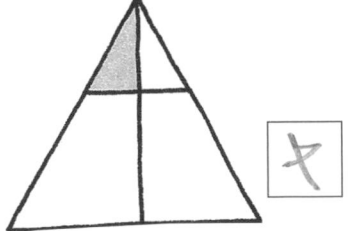 ✗

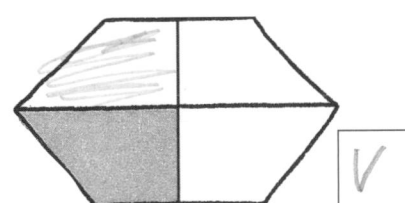 ✓

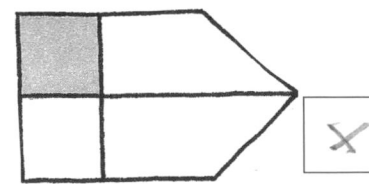 ✗

Colour one-quarter ($\frac{1}{4}$).

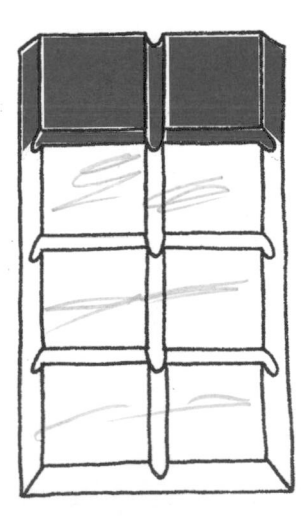 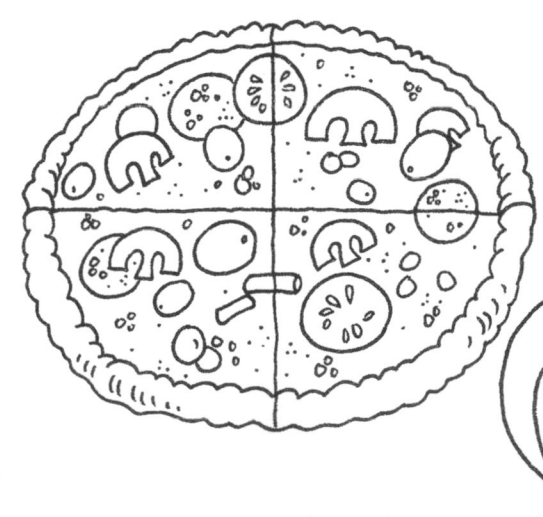 

21

Adding up

Count the beads.

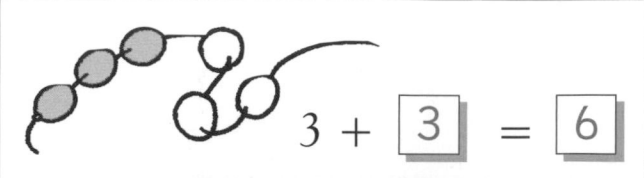

3 + 3 = 6

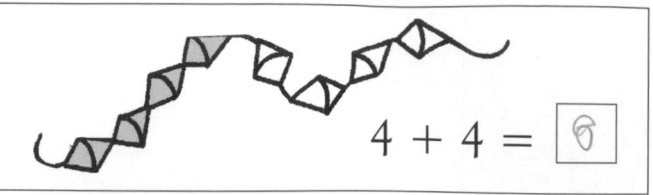

4 + 4 = 8

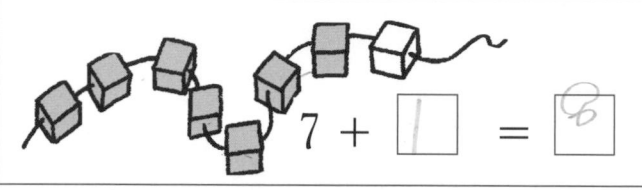

7 + 1 = 8

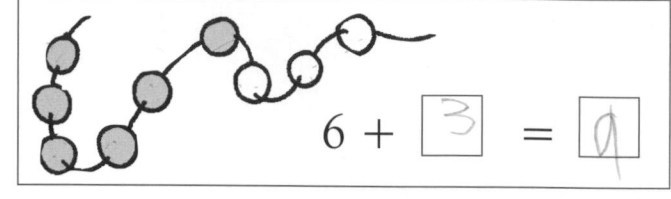

6 + 3 = 9

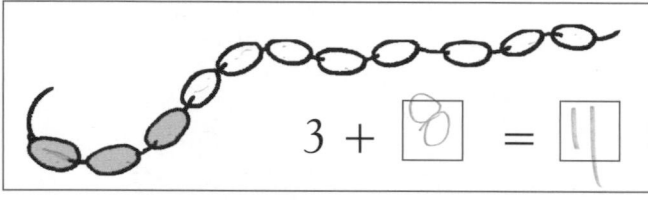

3 + 8 = 11

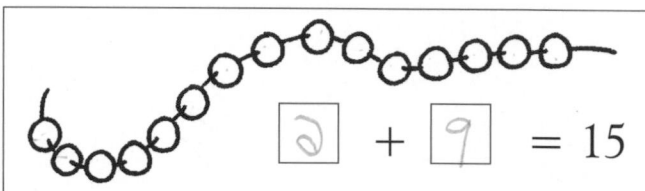

2 + 9 = 15

Count on.

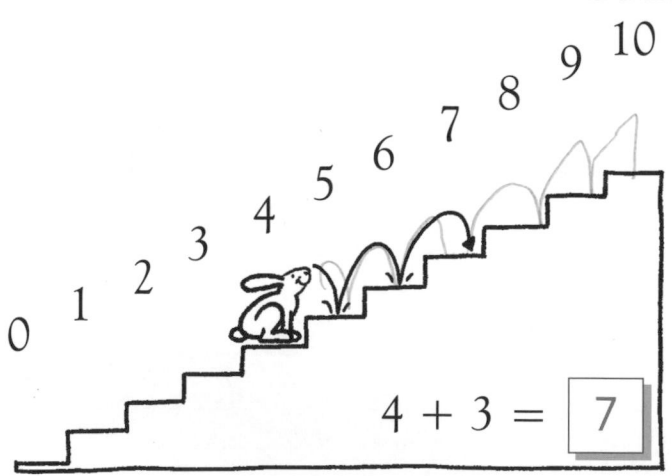

4 + 3 = 7

2 + 7 = 9

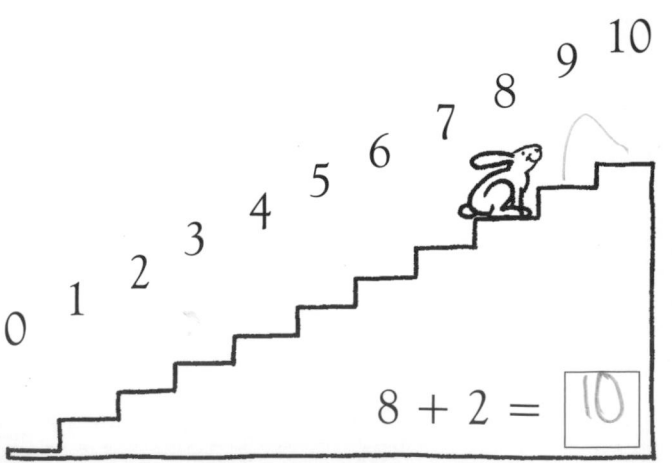

8 + 2 = 10

5 + 5 = 10

Adding animals

Count and add the animals, then write the number.

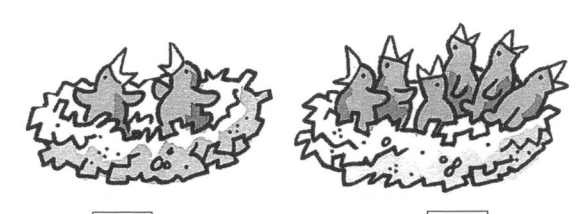
2 and 6 → 8

7 and 7 → 15

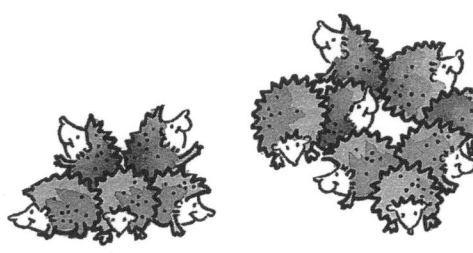
5 and 2 → 12

8 and 4 → 4

9 and 3 → 12

6 and 4 → 9

Write the missing numbers in the boxes.

7 and 4 → 11   3 and 9 → 12   6 and 6 → 12

9 + 5 → 14   2 + 8 → 10   3 + 11 → 14

9 and 3 → 12   6 and 4 → 10   13 and 4 → 17

2 + 3 → 5   16 + 0 → 16   15 + 4 → 19

Taking away

Cross out the animals and write the answers.

$4 - 1 \longrightarrow \boxed{3}$

$6 - 2 \longrightarrow \boxed{4}$

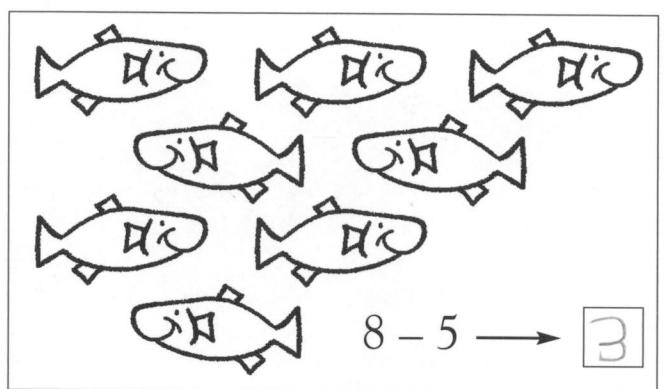

$8 - 5 \longrightarrow \boxed{3}$

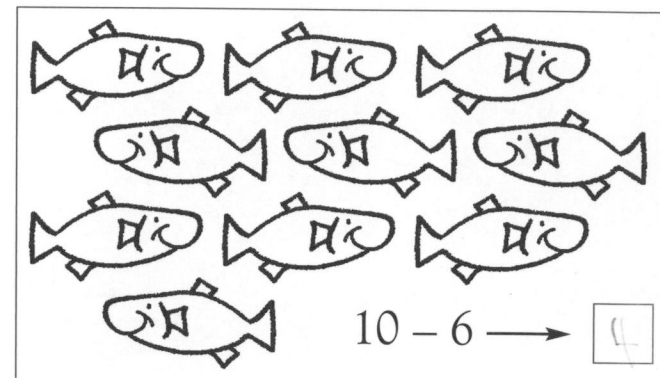

$10 - 6 \longrightarrow \boxed{4}$

Cross out the fruits and write the answers.

$8 - 3 = \boxed{2}$

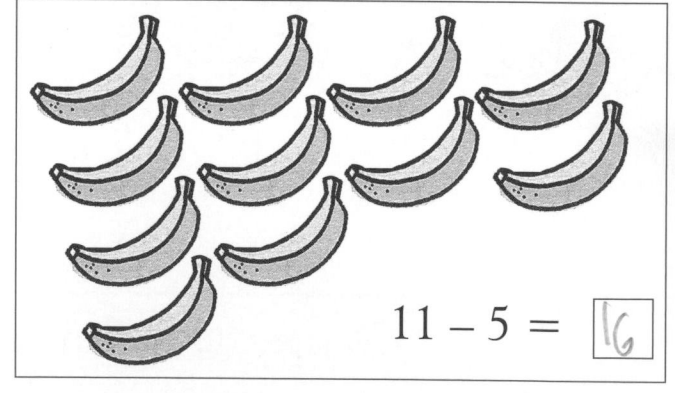

$11 - 5 = \boxed{6}$

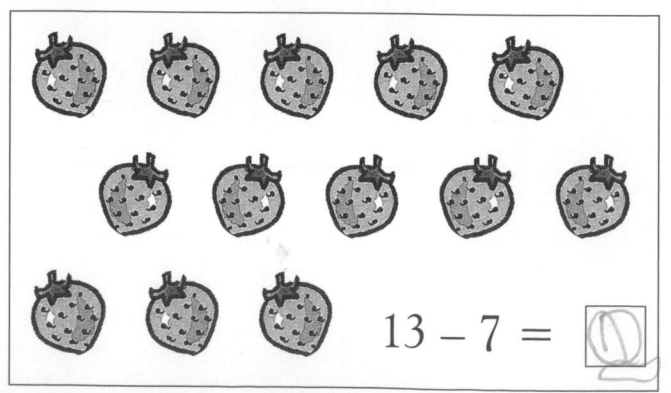

$13 - 7 = \boxed{0}$

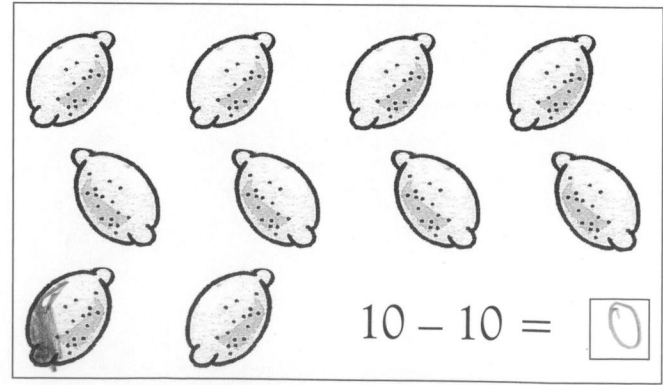

$10 - 10 = \boxed{0}$

Counting back

Count back.

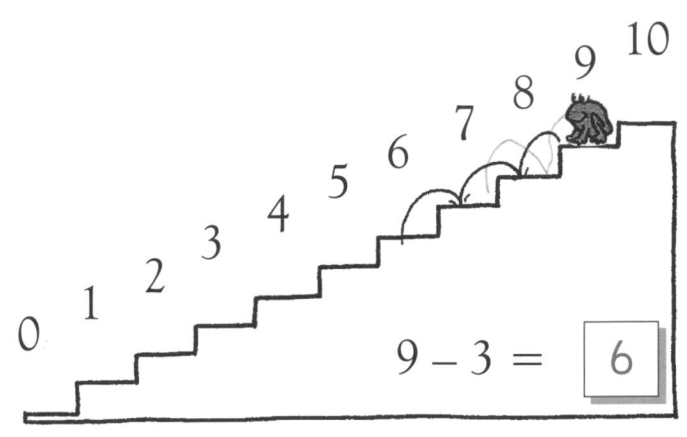

$9 - 3 = \boxed{6}$

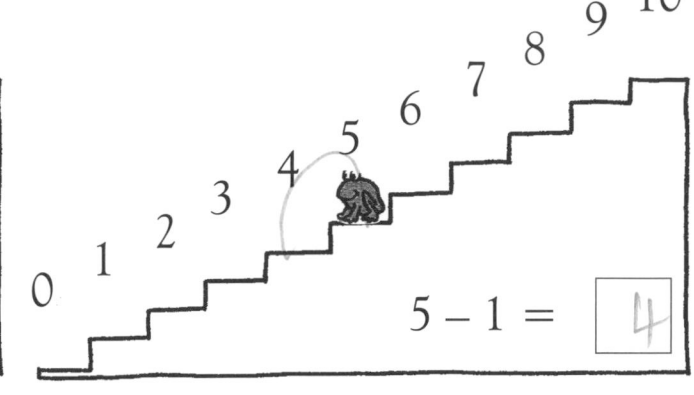

$5 - 1 = \boxed{4}$

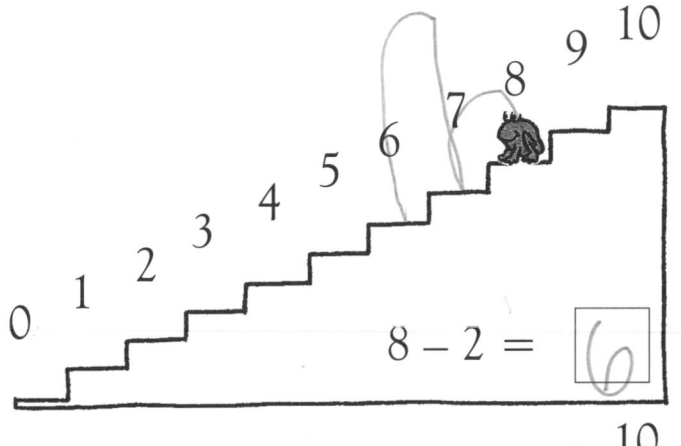

$8 - 2 = \boxed{6}$

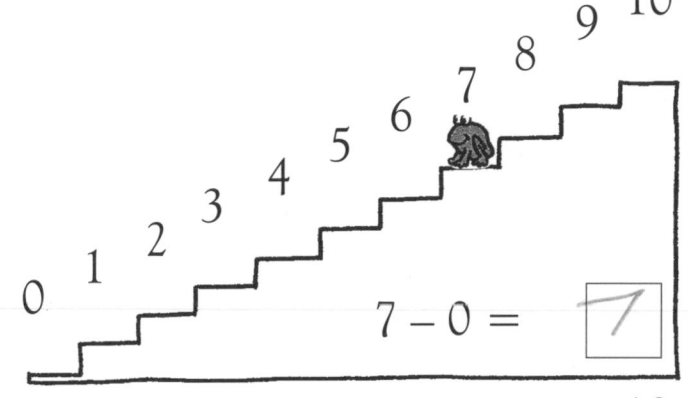

$7 - 0 = \boxed{7}$

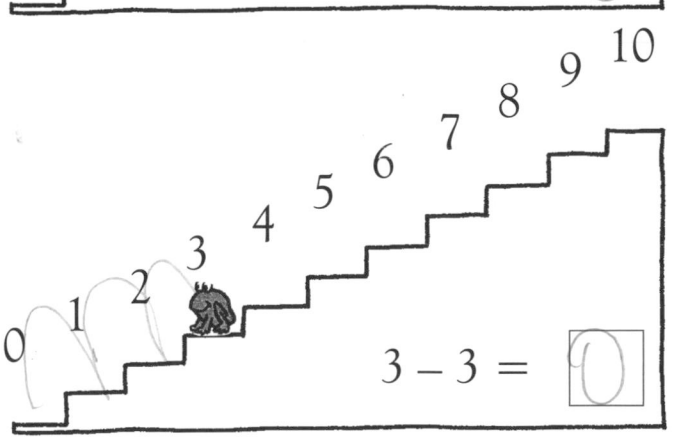

$3 - 3 = \boxed{0}$

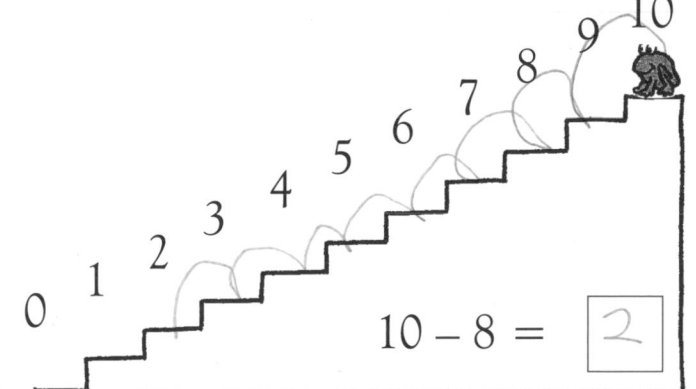

$10 - 8 = \boxed{2}$

Write the missing numbers in the boxes.

$3 - 3 = \boxed{0}$ $20 - 10 = \boxed{10}$ $9 - \boxed{6} = 6$ $15 - \boxed{10} = 5$

$5 - 4 = \boxed{1}$ $8 - 8 = \boxed{0}$ $5 - \boxed{5} = 0$ $20 - \boxed{20} = 4$

$15 - 4 = \boxed{10}$ $19 - 9 = \boxed{10}$ $6 - \boxed{6} = 2$ $18 - \boxed{10} = 11$

$10 - 9 = \boxed{1}$ $16 - 9 = \boxed{10}$ $13 - \boxed{3} = 10$ $10 - \boxed{10} = 4$

Lots of

Write the missing numbers in the boxes.

  | 2 | lots of | 3 | ⟶ | 6 |

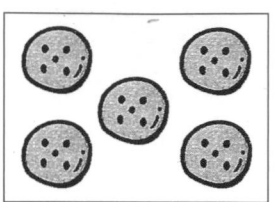 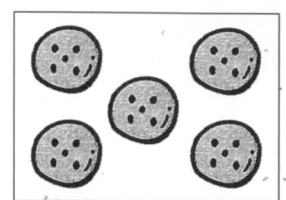 | 2 | lots of | 5 | ⟶ | 7 |

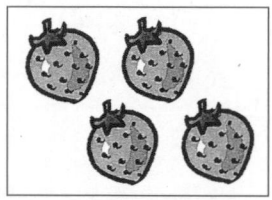 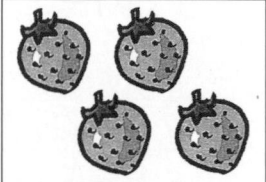 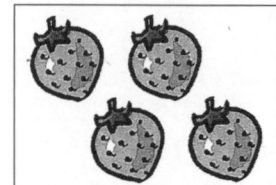 | 3 | lots of | 4 | ⟶ | 1 |

 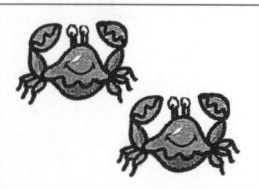  | R | lots of | 2 | ⟶ | 6 |

    | 2 | lots of | 2 | ⟶ | |

Draw your own pictures in the boxes.

   | 3 | lots of | 3 | ⟶ | 9 |

 | 2 | lots of | 4 | ⟶ | 8 |

Money

Which coin?

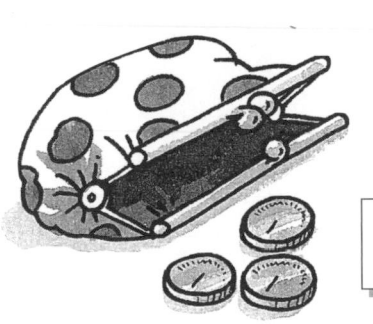  

How much?

 3p

 4p

  6P

 12P

 21P

 8 P

Put the money in the piggy bank.

 3p

 11p

 7p

27

Ordering stories

Write 1st, 2nd, or 3rd.

 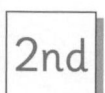 2nd
 3rd
 1st

  3rd
  1st
  2nd

 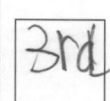 3rd
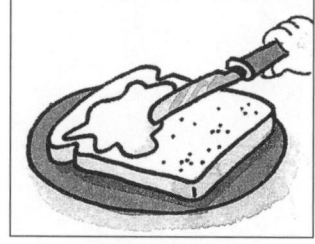 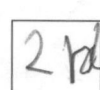 2nd
 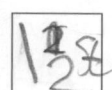 1st

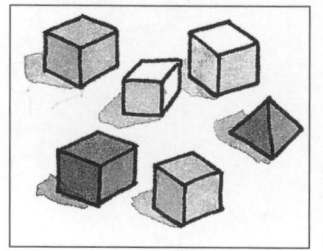 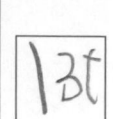 1st
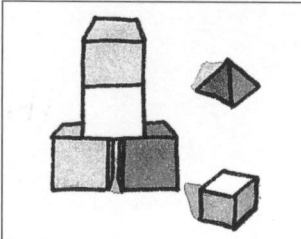  2nd
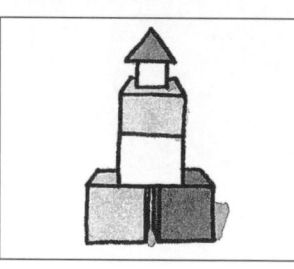  3rd

Draw a line to 1st, 2nd, 3rd, or 4th.

4th   **2nd**   **1st**   **3rd**

Time

Write the times in the boxes.

 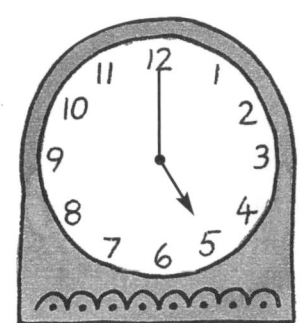  

`3` o'clock   `5` o'clock   `8` o'clock   `⎜⎜` o'clock

Draw the hands on the clock faces.

4 o'clock   10 o'clock   1 o'clock   6 o'clock

Match the times to the clocks.

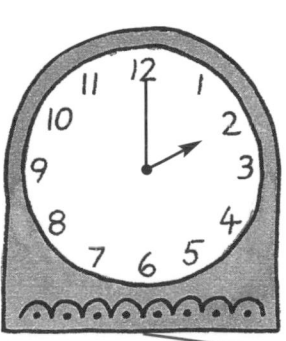   

12 o'clock   7 o'clock   2 o'clock   9 o'clock

Graphs

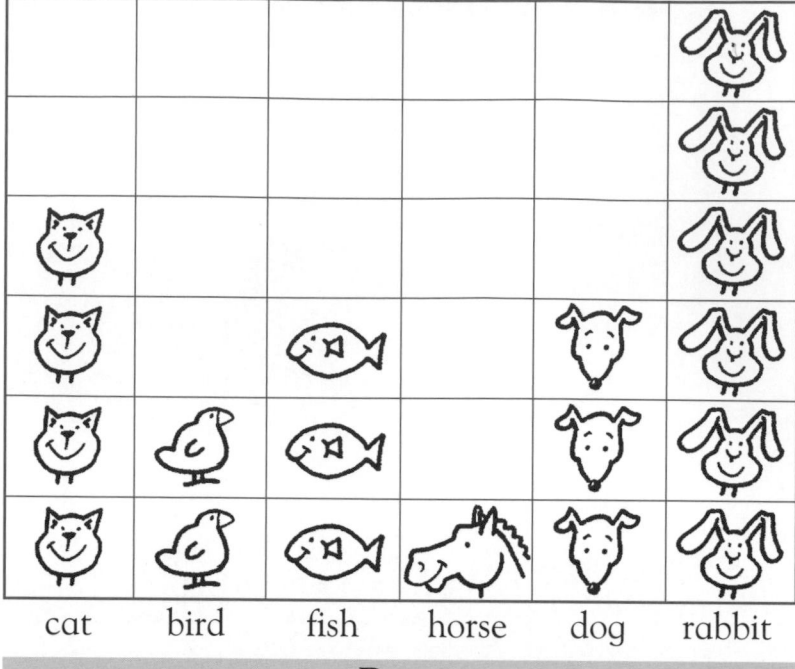

How many pets?

Which pet?

6   2    1

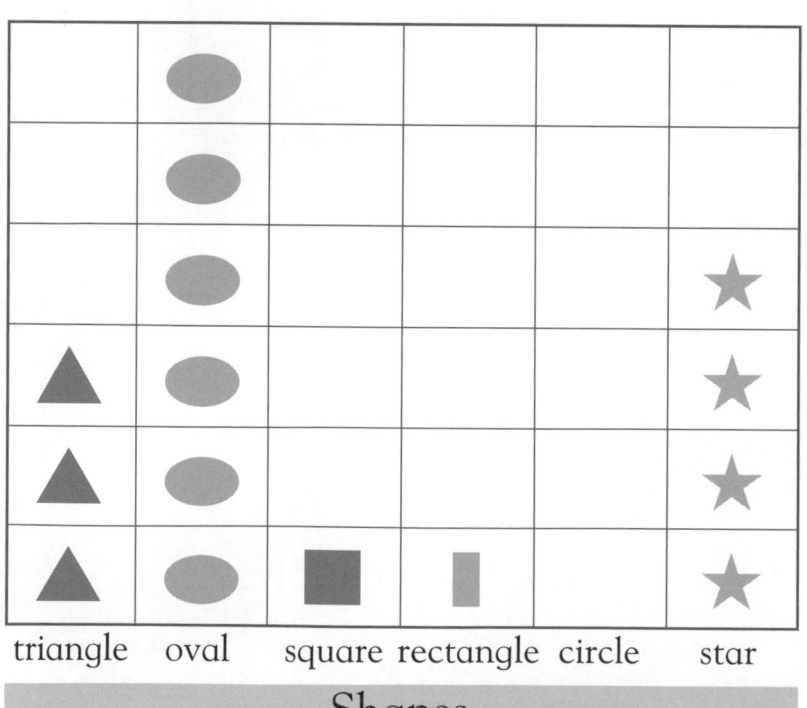

How many shapes?

Which shape?

4    0    3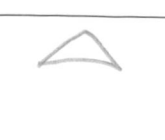

30

2D shapes

= yellow	 = green	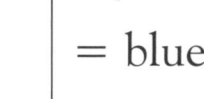 = purple		= blue

Colour the shapes.

Colour the shapes.

How many?

 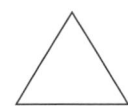  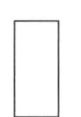

How many?

 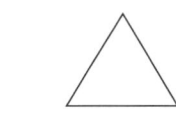  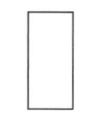

  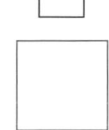

Make a picture.

How many?

   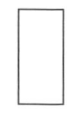

  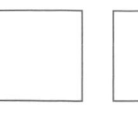

3D shapes

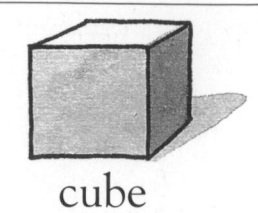 cube 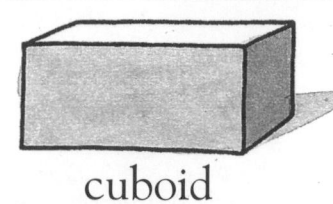 cuboid  sphere 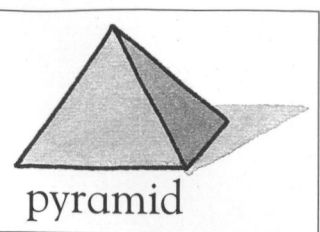 pyramid

Match the shapes to the names.

 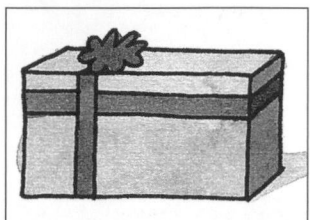 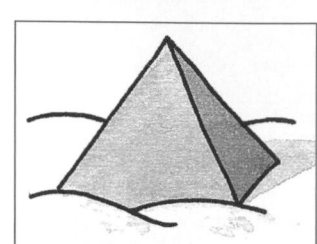 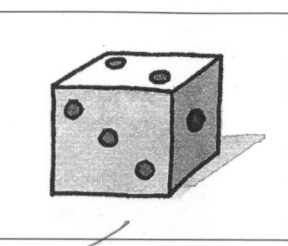

pyramid sphere cube cuboid

How many?

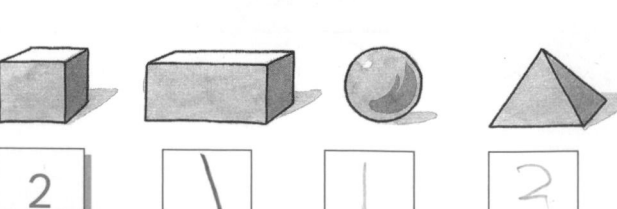

| 2 | 1 | 1 | 2 |

How many?

| 3 | 5 | | 5 |